2,00/9

Streisand
The Pictorial Biography

Streisand
The Pictorial Biography

Diana Karanikas Harvey and Jackson Harvey

COURAGE
BOOKS
AN IMPRINT OF RUNNING PRESS
PHILADELPHIA • LONDON

A Running Press Book

© 1997 by Michael Friedman Publishing Group, Inc.

Printed in Hong Kong by Wing King Tong Company Limited.

9 8 7 6 5 4 3 2 1

Digit on the right indicates the number of this printing

Library of Congress Cataloging-in-Publication Number 96-71608

ISBN 0-7624-0069-2

Streisand
The Pictorial Biography
was prepared and produced by
Michael Friedman Publishing Group, Inc.
15 West 26th Street
New York, New York 10010

Editor: Stephen Slaybaugh
Designer: Andrea Karman
Photography Editor: Wendy Missan
Production Director: Karen Matsu Greenberg

Color separations by HK Scanner Arts Int'l Ltd.

Published by Courage Books, an imprint of
Running Press Book Publishers
125 South Twenty-second Street
Philadelphia, Pennsylvania 19103-4399

Dedication

This book is dedicated to Frances Reed, our beloved Granny Franny.

Acknowledgments

We gratefully acknowledge the following:

Stephen Slaybaugh, Alex and Helen Karanikas, John and Sarah Harvey, George Leis, and all

the nice people on the eighteenth floor.

CONTENTS

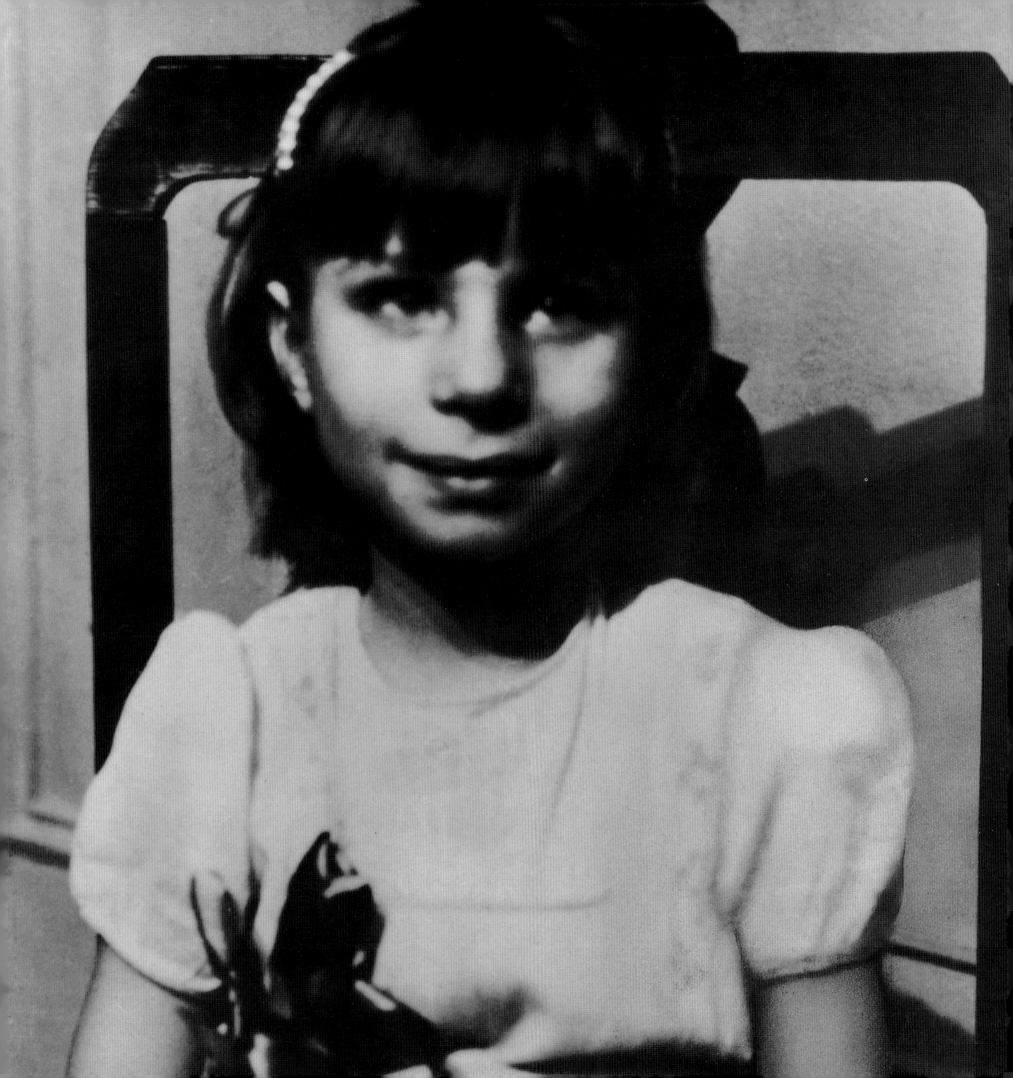

ONE

Funny Girl

S he was born Barbara Joan Streisand on April 24, 1942, in Brooklyn, New York. While a brutal world war raged overseas, her parents, Emanuel and Diana Streisand, both descendants of Jewish immigrants, were filled with elation. For seven years, since the birth of their son Sheldon in 1935, the Streisands, especially Diana, had dreamed of having a daughter. On that day, their prayers were answered and their little family became complete. None of them could have known that their lives soon would be shattered by tragedy.

Manny Streisand, an athletic man with seemingly boundless energy, was handsome and intelligent. "He was an adventurer," Barbra (who later changed the spelling of her name) once said of her father. He was respected and well liked by all who knew him, and most important of all, he deeply loved his family and would do anything necessary to provide for them. At the time of Barbara's birth, Manny had already received his master's degree in education and was teaching English at George Westinghouse Vocational High School in Brooklyn. In the spring of 1943, he decided to take a summer job as a counselor at Camp Cascade in Highmount, New York, to help cover the expenses related to the arrival of his new daughter.

From the moment her husband accepted the summer position, Diana Streisand was apprehensive about the trip: it meant packing the whole family up and spending the entire season in the Catskill mountains, far away from the Brooklyn flat she so loved. More importantly, the job would be extremely strenuous for her thirty-five-year-old husband. While Manny seemed perfectly healthy, Diana knew something was not right. In 1930, after their wedding, Diana and Manny had driven into Manhattan for their honeymoon. On the way back, a car in front of them braked unexpectedly and their car smashed into it, slamming Manny's head into the windshield. Since the accident he had suffered from chronic headaches. Then, in 1935, several months after Sheldon was born, Manny had fallen to the floor in a fit of convulsions and passed out. The doctor said he had had an epileptic seizure brought on by the head injury, and a seizure could happen again at any time.

Still, Manny and his family traveled north to Camp Cascade for the two-month stint. The job was more arduous than he had anticipated; he had to hike, play games, and manage the activities of more than 150 children. He was constantly exhausted and his headaches became

Page 8: "She was a demon as a little girl, I could never stop her from what she wanted to do, because she was always ready to jump into something and carry it out on her own." —Diana Kind on her daughter, Barbara Streisand.

Page 9: As a teenager, Barbara was often ostracized for her unusual looks. Eventually, however, she would use them to her advantage.

more intense. On a hot, humid day in August, Manny's headache became so intense that he had to lie down to rest, and he passed out. Diana, unable to revive him, rushed him to a small local hospital. He was pronounced dead several hours later. On that afternoon, August 4, 1943, little Barbara's life was changed forever.

A distraught Diana, penniless and still in shock, moved herself, Barbara, and Sheldon into her parents' apartment on Pulaski Street in Brooklyn. The tiny three-room apartment was cramped and uncomfortable. Diana's parents, the Rosens, slept in one bed, with Diana and Barbara in another, plus Sheldon on a fold-out cot near the dining room table. There was no living room, no couch. Barbra would later recall, "Couches were to me, like, what rich people had." More disturbing, as Sheldon later related, "There was no love in that house." The Rosens were cold and undemonstrative, and Diana was so traumatized by the death of her husband that she was unable to express anything but grief. Barbra has said, "Emotionally, my mother left me at the same time [as my father]." Diana also literally left her daughter, to go to work as a bookkeeper in downtown Brooklyn. Barbara would cry and throw a tantrum every time her mother left for work, so

afraid was she that her only living parent would also desert her. When Diana finally returned home, she was too exhausted and dejected to pay any mind to her energetic and inquisitive daughter.

Naturally, Barbara found ways to entertain herself. She played tea party and dress-up. She spent hours in front of the mirror, experimenting with her mother's makeup. Once she smeared lipstick all over her face and a blanket, much to her grandmother's dismay. Another time, she tried to shave with her grandfather's razor, cutting herself and prompting a trip to the hospital. She also spent hours singing in the halls of her apartment building. "Barbara started to sing as early as she could talk," her mother remembers. While some of the neighbors were annoyed, others were so delighted that when little Barbara stopped, they would beg her to sing some more.

Eager to get the rambunctious Barbara out of the house, Diana sent her five-year-old daughter off to grade school at the yeshiva on Willoughby Street in Brooklyn. Terrified at first, Barbara soon came to enjoy school as a respite from her dismal home. After school, Barbara would go over to a kindly neighbor's house. That neighbor, Tobey Borokow, not only had a

Barbra's mother, Diana. Barbra still seeks her hard-won approval.

Barbara was devastated when her mother, concerned over her five-year-old daughter's lack of appetite and resultant thin and gangly appearance, insisted on sending her away to summer "health camp." Upon her arrival at camp, Barbara was subjected to a horrible bathing. According to Barbra, "I remember their taking off my clothes and dumping me into this bath like I was a piece of dirt. They scrubbed me and washed me and put this lice disinfectant in my hair, then they put me into their uniform." She cried so frequently in the ensuing weeks that the other children made fun of her, to which she responded that her tears were caused by a malfunctioning tear duct. She also developed a psychosomatic asthma condition. A hypochondriac, Barbra has suffered from psychological illnesses her entire life.

Barbara was sent to the health camp for two miserable summers. In the months between, she spent much of her time playing with Irving Borokow, whom she described years later as "my first boyfriend." The pair played house and ran a lemonade stand together. Barbara continued at the yeshiva and, at the age of seven, had her first taste of performing when she sang in the yeshiva PTA's assembly program. She practiced intensely for her

son who went to school with Barbara, but she also owned a wondrous item that the Streisands didn't have—a television set. Barbara and Tobey's son, Irving, would watch anything they could, but were especially fond of Laurel and Hardy. Despite its tiny seven-and-a-half-inch screen, that television captivated Barbara, opening her eyes and imagination to a world of laughter and excitement, a world that was the complete opposite of her own. The television provided Barbara's earliest inspiration to become an actress.

performance, but when the big day arrived, she came down with a terrible cold. Diana put her back in bed and told her to forget about singing that day. Barbara was furious. Her mother remembered, "She leaped out of bed, put on her new dress, which hung on her like a rag because she was so skinny, and went to the meeting. Cold or no cold, she sang." After the performance, an excited Barbara ran up to her mother and asked her what she thought. Her mother responded, "Your arms are too thin." Then Diana took her daughter home and put her back in bed. Despite her mother's response, Barbara had felt the thrill of performing before a live audience for the first time.

During that summer, the summer of 1949, Barbara was sent off to Hebrew health camp, which was as odious to her as the previous one. In the middle of the summer, though, something happened that was even more traumatic to the little girl than going to camp.

For some time her mother, then forty years old, had been dating, looking to remarry. Barbara hated all the suitors and cried vehemently when they came to pick Diana up, fearing her mother would never return. When she saw her mother being kissed, she thought the man was killing her, despite the fact that Diana

was laughing. So when one of those suitors, Louis Kind, accompanied her mother to camp that summer, Barbara was notably unhappy. Louis Kind—an Orthodox Jew with a background in the garment industry, the owner of several rooming houses, and a self-proclaimed lover of children—was sixteen years older than Diana. He was also separated from his first wife, but still, to Barbara's mother, he seemed a good catch. To Barbara, though, he seemed particularly repulsive, no doubt because his visit to camp indicated a serious relationship and that he might be a stand-in for her irreplaceable father. Barbara behaved miserably during his stay, and when Diana and Louis packed up to go back home, Barbara threw an ugly tantrum and declared, "You're not leaving here without me!" Her mother finally acquiesced and the three drove home in complete silence.

Despite Louis' efforts to win Barbara over—he even bought her a doll, whose head she ripped off—the little girl refused to accept him. Still, Louis continued his pursuit of Diana, and she accepted his advances even though marriage did not seem to be on Kind's agenda. Though his divorce was final, Kind did not want to jump into another marriage, especially not one that included the responsibility of two more children (he already had three of his own), one of whom hated him. Even when Diana approached him with the news that she was pregnant by him, Louis Kind balked at marrying her. Mortified, Diana, who was still living in her parents' house, tried to keep the pregnancy a secret, but when she no longer could, her father immediately kicked her and her children out of his home.

Diana moved her family into a one-bedroom apartment in the Vanderveer Estates in the Flatbush area of Brooklyn. The complex was cold and ugly but it was new and in a decent neighborhood, and the rent was cheap. Barbara, however, was devastated. In leaving the old apartment, she was also separated from her friend Irving Borokow and his mother, Tobey, who had became something of a surrogate mother to Barbara. Since Diana could no longer afford to send her to yeshiva school, Barbara would have to switch to Public School 89, which was directly across the street from the new complex. All the upheavals in her life left the little girl so distraught that, after the first night in the new apartment, she awoke with a clicking sound in her ears that wouldn't go away. Her mother brushed it off, but Barbara was convinced that something was wrong.

"From that day," Barbra remembers, "I led a whole secret life."

Finally, in December 1950, when Diana was nine months pregnant, Louis Kind changed his mind and the two were married by a justice of the peace. A couple of weeks later, Diana gave birth to a daughter, Rosalind. While Kind doted on his new daughter, every other aspect of the marriage was a complete disaster from the outset. He refused financial support to the family, claiming he had no money; he disappeared for days at a time, then fought bitterly with Diana when he returned; and he verbally abused Sheldon and Barbara, disparaging Barbara's looks both in private and in front of her friends. In time, he began to physically abuse Diana on a regular basis.

Barbara lapsed into her own world. Her hypochondria intensified; she was at one time convinced she had cancer, at another time a heart condition. She developed tinnitus, or a ringing in the ears, and wore scarves around her head to try to block out the sound.

Her fantasy world also secured the foundation for her future endeavors. She spent hours in front of the television—the one benefit of Louis Kind's arrival—loving even the commercials, mimicking the actors and actresses, and dream-

Barbra with her brother Sheldon and half-sister Roslyn (who, like Barbra, changed the spelling of her name) backstage at the Grand Finale in New York in 1977. At the time, Roslyn was performing to standing room only audiences.

ing of the glamorous lives of the stars. She planted herself in front of the bathroom mirror, studying her face, experimenting with makeup, and elegantly smoking her mother's cigarettes. And she sang—in the halls of the apartment building, at school, anywhere she could. By the time she was ten years old, she was doggedly set on being a performer. Her entertainment aspirations were known to the few new friends she made in public school; even back then, one of her friends recalled, "She was very intense about it." While her mother balked at Barbara's

show business ambitions, primarily because she thought her daughter wasn't pretty enough to be successful, little Barbara was adamant. She took ballet lessons for six months, sang and danced in a hotel talent show, and even auditioned for the Metro Goldwyn Mayer motion picture studio, whose talent scouts were seeking kiddy talent. When the scouts offered Barbara a spot in their training classes, Diana refused to let her daughter participate because there was no pay. She did, however, allow Barbara to participate in a talent contest while on summer

STREISAND, BARBARA
Freshman Chorus, 1, 2; Choral
Club, 2-4.

*Barbara's high
school yearbook photo.
Erasmus Hall
High School's grad-
uates also included
such performers as
Neil Sedaka and
Neil Diamond.*

In September 1955, Barbara entered Erasmus Hall High School in Brooklyn, an institution with a sprawling college-type campus and a freshman class of thirteen hundred students. Erasmus Hall was known for its superior academic standards, and Barbara, who had been a member of P.S. 89's Intellectually Gifted Opportunity program, was put directly into honors classes. She excelled academically in the first half of her freshman year, with a grade point average in the top three percent of her class. Socially, though, she didn't fit in. Classmates called her "a loner" and "aloof," and her homeroom teacher said that she was "self-centered." While she did develop several close friendships at Erasmus Hall, she made no real effort to be popular with her fellow students; her mind was on other things.

One of those things was her part-time job at Choy's Chinese restaurant, where she worked after school. Mr. and Mrs. Choy, whom Barbara had befriended several years earlier, were a surrogate family to the young woman. Barbara soaked up their culture, clothing herself in silk kimonos, wearing her hair piled in a bun, and growing her nails long and painting them bright red. Barbara's fabulous nails have since remained one of her trademarks. Mrs. Choy

vacation at a hotel in the Catskill mountains. Barbara won the contest and so impressed the hotel guests that two of them asked her to sing at weddings for a small salary. "Y'see, Ma," she proclaimed, "I can make money at this!" When she returned home, though, thirteen-year-old Barbara was met not only with the dismal prospect of facing her abusive stepfather, but with a brand-new and, in its own way, frightening challenge: high school.

answered the questions for Barbara that she could never even ask her mother: "about love, life, and sex," Barbra recalls. The Choys were also the first people to capture Barbara on film. In a home movie of a birthday party, Barbara covers her face and ducks her head every time the camera turns to her.

While Barbara didn't participate in many extracurricular activities in her first few months of high school, there was one group she was adamant about being involved with: the Erasmus Choral Club. The chorus accepted only the most talented students and was led by the handsome Cosimo DePietto, whom Barbara, as well as many of the other girls, had a crush on. Barbara auditioned twice for the choir in the space of several months, and was twice rejected. "I never knew her to have any

Barbra celebrates the openning of A Star Is Born with her old friends and former employers, the Choys, at Tavern on the Green in New York City.

particular or outstanding talent," DePietto said years later. Still, with characteristic determination, Barbara was bound to be accepted, so she took up an offer she had had from a pianist at the Catskills Hotel to record a professional tape of her singing. With the tape complete, she again approached DePietto. He finally acquiesced, but Barbara was put in the last row of the choir and was never allowed a solo. She quit after two years, partly because of DePietto's inability to recognize her talent, but mostly due to the fact that she had moved on to far more challenging endeavors.

In April 1956, Barbara had an inspirational experience when her mother, for Barbara's fourteenth birthday, allowed her to go into Manhattan to see a production of *The Diary of Anne Frank*. The experience so moved Barbara that she came home with a new plan. "I could play Anne Frank," she told her mother. "I knew what she was feeling!" Determined to be an actress, Barbara instantly began auditioning. Only days after the play, she attended an audition for the leading role in Otto Preminger's film version of Bernard Shaw's play *Saint Joan*. While the casting people said her reading was excellent, Preminger eventually cast the typically beautiful Jean Seberg in the role. Barbara

was devastated. Her mother's notion that Barbara would never make it as an actress because she was so unconventional-looking was confirmed by the incident, and Diana began actively dissuading her daughter from further pursuit of an acting career.

In the meantime, Diana's life was again in upheaval. In May 1956, Louis Kind moved out for good and a bitter divorce proceeding began. Even though Diana was awarded some support money in the settlement, it wasn't nearly enough, and the family's financial situation became even worse. Barbara found herself making do with unstylish clothing and, because Diana went back to work, frequently baby-sitting her half-sister Rosalind. Barbara loved Rosalind, whom she saw as her opposite; Rosalind was chubby and cute, while Barbara felt skinny and plain.

With her mother working, Barbara was free to spend her time as she pleased, and she spent much of her spare time at the movies, again indulging her fantasy world of glamour and stardom. She also continued to pursue the acting career that her mother was so opposed to. The summer after her sophomore year, Barbara lied about her age and spent the money earmarked for her college education to participate in a summer acting apprenticeship at Malden Bridge Playhouse in Malden Bridge, New York. Despite Diana's disapproval, she allowed her daughter to go. Barbara received her first reviews that summer for her performance as a sex-crazed secretary in *The Desk Set*, and they were favorable. One local paper called her "a fine young comedienne," while another said she turned in "a fine performance."

Then, at the beginning of her junior year in high school, Barbara got what would turn out to be a pivotal break in her burgeoning career. She was accepted into a year-round apprenticeship program at the Cherry Lane Theater in Greenwich Village. Her mother had not even been aware that Barbara had taken the subway into Manhattan to audition, and she only allowed her daughter to participate after she promised to keep her grades up at school.

Barbara did manage to keep her grades up as she met the people who would help to nurture not only her burgeoning talent, but her blossoming womanhood as well. During her internship, she met Allan Miller, a Manhattan acting coach. Although he labeled Barbara's audition for his classes as "the worst I've ever seen in my life," her enthusiasm, inquisitiveness, and forceful personality convinced him to allow her

into his class. She became very close to Miller and his wife, Anita, who was also an actress. Much to Diana's dismay, Barbara would spend nights over at the Millers' house, learning or merely having fun. Before long, under Miller's tutelage, she was the star of the class.

Barbara also became involved with her first boyfriend, an aspiring actor named Roy Scott. It was with Scott that Barbara had her first sexual experience. It was no surprise that when Diana found out, she became hysterical with disapproval. She called the Millers and accused them of ruining her

Barbra with Roslyn at the Plaza Hotel for Roslyn's engagement party in 1969. Louis Kind always considered his daughter Roslyn the pretty one.

Barbra performs at New York's Bon Soir club in 1962.

daughter's life, and even called Scott's parents to voice her dismay. Scott later recalled, "Her mother tried to control her too much, to protect her too much. And yes, it hurt [my] relationship [with Barbara]."

Shortly before Christmas in her senior year of high school, Barbara auditioned for a role in a play called *Driftwood*, which was being produced at an off-Broadway venue called the Garret Theater. At seventeen years old, Barbara nabbed her first acting job in Manhattan. She was cast as the tough, thirty-five-year-old Lorna, playing opposite a young Joan Rivers (then Joan Molinsky). *Driftwood*, whose director was himself only seventeen, garnered not a single review and, much to Barbara's disappointment, closed after only six weeks.

On January 26, 1959, during *Driftwood's* run, Barbara graduated from high school with the fourth-best grade average in the class. Despite her strong academics and her mother's badgering, Barbara had no interest in college. Instead, just weeks after graduation, she packed her bags and moved to Manhattan, where she could wholeheartedly pursue her dream of stardom.

Barbara's dream was not long in coming true. She took all the obstacles her mother saw—her unconventional looks, her quirky personality, and her unique way of dressing—and, with a ferocious force of will, turned them to her advantage. Yet while Barbara was intent upon being an actress, it was her amazing vocal gift that first thrust her into the New York performance scene. By the time she was eighteen, she was already stunning audiences at clubs like the Lion and the Bon Soir in Manhattan, the Caucus Club in Detroit, and the Crystal Palace in St. Louis, as well as appearing regularly on *PM East*, Mike Wallace's late-night television talk/variety show. Barbara had already become such a hit in New York's gay community that, whenever she appeared on the show, gay clubs would offer two-for-one drinks.

She changed her name, eliminating the second, unpronounced vowel, and in doing so made it unique. She also met manager Marty Erlichman, and although the two never signed a contract and worked separately for nearly ten years (between 1977 and 1986), he still remains her manager today. While Erlichman initially set out to find Barbra singing engagements at more upscale clubs, he also whole-

heartedly believed in her as an actress, and before long she was cast in the off-Broadway revue *An Evening with Harry Stoones*. Barbra's reviews were unanimously good, but the show's weren't, and it closed soon after its opening. Still, Erlichman did not give up on his nineteen-year-old client, nor did Barbra give up on herself. Erlichman successfully negotiated a stint for her at the swank Blue Angel club, and on the morning before she opened, he secured her an audition for a new Broadway musical produced by the renowned David Merrick (*Gypsy*) called *I Can Get It for You Wholesale*. This audition was the beginning of the whirlwind that sent Barbra skyrocketing into stardom at an astounding pace—astounding, that is, to everyone but Marty Erlichman. When Erlichman first saw her at the Bon Soir club, he had told her, "Barbra, the first time out of the box, you're going to win every award that this business has to offer: the Tony, the Grammy, the Oscar... you're going to be the biggest movie star of them all." Barbra responded, with a laugh, "I think I'm going to be a star too." While his was only a bit of an overstatement, hers was a drastic understatement. Barbra was indeed on the verge of becoming a superstar.

TWO

A Star Is Born

arbra Streisand walked onto the stage of the St. James Theater on November 16, 1961, to audition for the director, the author, and the composer of *I Can Get It for You Wholesale*. From the moment she appeared before them, the production staff knew they were in for something—they just didn't know quite what. She wore a tattered fur-trimmed coat, tennis shoes, and a knit cap. Her hair was a mess, and she was loaded down with a plastic case full of sheet music and a bag of sandwiches. As she walked across the stage, she dropped the case and sheet music floated everywhere; when she went to pick it up, her bag got tangled in her coat sleeve. For any other performer, the situation would've been disastrous, but not for Barbra. She had her auditioners laughing already, unsure whether she was a comedic genius or a freak, and she had barely uttered a single word.

When she decided to speak, she said, "Listen, my name's Barbra Streisand. With only two 'a's. In the first name I mean. I figure that third 'a' in the middle, who needs it? What would ya like me to do?" After they had stopped laughing out loud, they told her to sing. "Sing?" she responded. "Even a jukebox you don't just say 'Sing.' You gotta first punch a button with the name of a song on it! What should I sing?" Thoroughly

intrigued, they told her to sing anything. Barbra continued her shtick by plopping down on a chair equipped with casters, taking her shoes off, removing a wad of gum from her mouth and sticking it under the chair, then careening across the stage while singing her audition song.

She was dazzling. They asked her back to audition for David Merrick, the famed Broadway producer. After she left and the magic had worn off, the director had his assistant check under the chair. There was no gum; her whole demeanor had been a brilliant act.

David Merrick needed to see her audition five times before he was convinced, barely, that she was the right choice for the role of Miss Marmelstein, which was originally written for an actress in her fifties. Not only did he find Barbra unattractive, but he thought she was downright weird. However, he finally gave in, and Barbra was cast in her first Broadway play.

From the outset of rehearsals Barbra behaved not like a nineteen-year-old in her first big show, but like a temperamental, demanding, and difficult superstar. She consistently showed up late, argued with the director, and refused to do a scene consistently, much to the chagrin of some of her fellow thespians. She even refused to be conventional in the bio she wrote for the

Page 22: Barbra posed for this shot at the beginning of her rise to superstardom in 1965.

Page 23: Streisand makes a grand entrance on her television special "Color Me Barbra."

Barbra receives a
congratulatory kiss
from Elliot at a
celebration party for
the cast of Funny
Girl, March 27,
1964.

program, in which she claimed she was born in Madagascar and raised in Rangoon. She explained, "I played the part of a Brooklyn girl. How boring it would have been to say I was from Brooklyn." Despite the complaints of the show's press agent, Barbra insisted, and the bio was published as she wrote it.

Her behavior did not endear her to Merrick. Barbra's tardiness led him to file a complaint with the stage union, Actor's Equity Association, before whom she appeared and apologized. Merrick was intent on replacing her during trial performances of the show, since he still found her too offbeat and quirky for a major Broadway production. Her amazing vocal talent combined with the strong backing of the show's composer kept her in. And Barbra was not the only performer in the show on Merrick's hit list. In fact, her rocky relationship with the producer helped to solidify her burgeoning romance with another actor Merrick was looking to fire (but never did)—the show's star, Elliot Gould.

One day after a rehearsal of Barbra's big number as Miss Marmelstein, the excited actress

Barbra onstage at the Shubert Theater as Miss Marmelstein in I Can Get it For You Wholesale.

and acting, and both being twenty-three years old, Elliot and Barbra had other similarities: their insecurities about their appearances, their Jewish faith, their Brooklyn upbringing, and their tough family lives (Elliot's parents, like Diana and Louis Kind, were constantly abusive to each other). Barbra remembers, "I was beginning to feel something for the guy, and it scared me half to death.... I guess I was in love."

I Can Get It for You Wholesale opened on Broadway on Thursday, March 22, 1962. Barbra brought the house down. When she uttered her final line, the audience awarded her a standing ovation that lasted three whole minutes. While the show received mixed reviews, the critics were uniform in their praise of Barbra's performance. Overnight, Barbra became the toast of the town. She appeared on the *Today* show, *Tonight* (later called *The Tonight Show*), *The Gary Moore Show*, and continued to appear regularly on *PM East*. She was also featured in *Life* magazine as one of its "Broadway Showstoppers," in *Mademoiselle* as "Most Likely to Succeed," and in the *New Yorker*, which labeled her a "coming star." She continued to perform at the Bon Soir, sang on the soundtrack albums for *Wholesale* and another musical, *Pins and Needles*, and secured a recording contract with the biggest

handed out her new phone number to all her cast members and announced, "Call me!" Only one responded that very evening. When Barbra picked up the phone, the male voice said, "You asked for somebody to call, so I called. I just wanted to say you were brilliant today. This is Elliot Gould." Then he hung up. Before long, Elliot and Barbra were dating and behaving like two lovestruck teenagers. They'd have snowball fights in the park, throw food at each other in restaurants, and giggle uncontrollably wherever they went. Beyond their love of watching movies

label at the time, Columbia Records. In her contract with Columbia, she maintained the ever-coveted "creative control" of her material. She was nominated for a Tony Award and won a New York Drama Critics Circle Award. The first time out, Barbra had become a star.

Wholesale ran for six months, in which time Barbra's relationship with Gould intensified, despite the fact that, in her supporting role, she was overwhelmingly more successful than he was as the star of the show. Gould moved into

Barbra's small bohemian apartment. Although they shared the space with a huge rat, which they named Gonzola, the two lovebirds were extremely happy. Gould recalled, "The happiest memories I have of Barbra are when we were living together before we were married. We were having a really romantic time."

When *I Can Get It for You Wholesale* closed on December 9, 1962, Barbra rushed backstage after the curtain went down and jubilantly cried, "I'm free! I'm free!" The actress had reason to

Fanny Brice was a strong-willed, comedic actress with a golden voice. Rarely has there been a part so ideally suited for its star. Barbra Streisand as Fanny Brice in Funny Girl.

be impatient; she was moving on to bigger and better things. She was preparing to appear on *The Ed Sullivan Show*; she was planning her first album; and she had beaten out several highly respected actresses to be cast in the starring role of a new Broadway musical. That musical was *Funny Girl*.

Funny Girl was based on the life of Fanny Brice, the famous comedienne and Ziegfeld Follies singing star. The story centers around her troubled romance and marriage to con man Nick Arnstein. The production was produced by the legendary Ray Stark (the son-in-law of Brice and Arnstein), and directed by Garson Kanin. The starring role of Fanny—a plain-looking Jewish woman, raised in New York City, with a prominent nose and a voice and comedic persona that made her famous—seemed tailor-made for Barbra. Jule Styne, the show's composer, was so convinced Barbra was the actress to play Fanny that he began writing songs designed for her voice before she was even set to play the role. After signing the contract in 1963, Barbra commented of her character, "We're very much alike. It's like me talking. Like Miss Brice, I find it hard to take advice from anyone."

In the months before rehearsals for *Funny Girl* began, Barbra became a recording star. Her first

Barbra stands in front of the mock marquee for the movie version of *Funny Girl*.

album, *The Barbra Streisand Album*, remained in the Top 40 for a stunning seventy-four weeks and went gold eighteen months after its release on February 25, 1963. Columbia quickly brought Barbra in to record another album. The album, aptly titled *The Second Barbra Streisand Album*, came out in August 1963 and jumped into the top ten on *Billboard's* chart in its first few weeks of release. The record stayed in the number two spot for three weeks and was certified gold after thirteen months.

The success of Barbra's albums was bolstered by diligent efforts to promote herself. In 1963, she toured from coast to coast, opening for the legendary Benny Goodman in New York and headlining at the famous star-studded Cocoanut Grove

Right: Barbra belts one out with Judy Garland and Ethel Merman on the CBS television program, The Judy Garland Show.

Right: Barbra's television career has been filled with many memorable performances and Emmy awards. Here she poses with her first Emmy, for "My Name Is Barbra," in 1965.

in Los Angeles. While in Hollywood, she signed with agents at CMA (now ICM), an agency possessing, among other strong points, a powerful motion pictures division. She also did a special performance in Washington, D.C., for President John F. Kennedy. Meanwhile, she continued appearing as a guest star on television, including an appearance on "The Bob Hope Comedy Special." Most notable, though, was her amazing and unforgettable performance with Judy Garland on *The Judy Garland Show*. So brilliant was Barbra that she was nominated for an Emmy Award for Best Variety Performance, the first time a guest star had ever received such an honor. *The Judy Garland Show* appearance was so special that, after it was over, Marty Erlichman told his client, "There's no more reason to be a guest artist on these cockamamie television shows. You just couldn't top that." Barbra didn't appear as a guest star for the next six years.

Somehow Barbra managed to find time in her busy schedule for romance. During an engagement in Lake Tahoe, where she was opening for Liberace, Barbra accepted a proposal of marriage from Elliot Gould. On Friday the thirteenth of September, Barbra and Elliot were married in Carson City. After the Tahoe stand, the two traveled to Barbra's next engagement, in

The Actress meets the President— Barbra with John F. Kennedy. Barbra has raised millions of dollars for Democratic candidates.

Los Angeles, where they stayed at the exclusive Beverly Hills Hotel, finding as much time as they could to behave like newlyweds on a honeymoon.

By the time rehearsals for *Funny Girl* commenced in December 1963, Barbra was riding high. Despite problems during the rehearsal period, Barbra's fights with Stark, and lack of a strong directorial hand from Kanin (Jerome Robbins was eventually brought in as "production supervisor" to whip the show into shape), when the musical opened at the Winter Garden Theater on March 26, 1964, Barbra took Broadway by storm. The show was a smash

success, driven by Barbra's astonishing performance. The critics raved: the *New York Times* said, "Barbra Streisand sets an entire theater ablaze.... she is the theater's new girl for all seasons."

In the weeks following the opening of *Funny Girl*, Barbra appeared on the covers of both *Time* and *Life* magazines. Her popularity grew to such an extent that women everywhere began doing their hair as she did, applying their eye makeup just like hers, and dressing in the same types of clothes she wore in order to achieve the Streisand "look." Barbra was finally liberated from the

Hello, Louis!—Louis Armstrong and Barbra hold the Grammys they won for Best Record Vocal Performances by a Male and Female, respectively. Barbra won for her recording of "People" and Armstrong for his recording of "Hello, Dolly."

little girl whose mother had chastised her for being too skinny and whose stepfather had ridiculed her as too ugly, and the young woman whose early detractors had hated her quirky looks and ugly clothes. Barbra was an idol, yet she was strangely unhappy.

"The reality can never live up to the fantasy, can it?" she asked a reporter. "The excitement of life lies in the hope, in the striving for something rather than the attainment." She was besieged by fans to the point of distraction, yet her family continually disappointed her. Louis Kind came

to see the show, but although Barbra waited backstage for over an hour, he never went back to see her, and only sent Barbra a dish of candy. She kept the dish until 1987. Her mother never praised her daughter to her face. Barbra said, "I wish I could convince my mother I'm a success. Even today she calls me and says, 'So-and-so in the office read something about you in the papers.' But it never seems to mean anything to her personally."

Gould also had problems with her popularity. Not only had all his acting endeavors failed to

Barbra talked to the
animals in her 1966
television special,
"Color Me Barbra."

A
Star Is
Born
33

win him any notoriety, but his claim to fame was emerging as playing the role of "Mr. Streisand." Still, he was stunned by Barbra's lack of enthusiasm for her newfound popularity and he commented, "The trouble with Barbra is that she can't seem to let herself be happy." All in all, superstardom didn't mean smooth sailing for Barbra. Her success, coupled with her strong personality, so daunted her co-star Sidney Chaplin that he developed a strong hatred of Barbra, which eventually prompted him to mutter obscenities to her under his breath during

scenes of the play. (He left the show in June 1965 and was replaced by Johnny Desmond.)

Still, Barbra plunged into more work, gaining further exposure, popularity, and professional accolades as she progressed. In February 1964, *Barbra Streisand/The Third Album* was released and quickly rose to number five on the charts. In April, the soundtrack for *Funny Girl* came out and climbed to *Billboard's* number two position. One month later, Barbra was awarded the Grammy for Best Female Vocalist for her first album, which also won the Grammy

Barbra holds Jason,
her newborn son by
Elliot Gould.

for Album of the Year. At twenty-one, she was (and still is) the youngest performer ever to win both awards in the same year. Her fourth album, *People*, was released in September and knocked the Beatles' *A Hard Day's Night* out of the top spot, giving Barbra a number one album. *People* won her a second consecutive Grammy for Best Female Vocalist.

Her first two television specials, "My Name is Barbra" (April 1965) and "Color Me Barbra" (March 1966), garnered huge ratings and fabulous reviews. The former was nominated for six Emmy Awards and won five, including Outstanding Individual Achievement by an Actor or Performer.

On December 29, 1966 Barbra gave birth to a son, Jason Emanuel Gould. She later said of giving birth, "It's a miracle, the height of creativity for any woman." Now the Goulds were a family.

Clearly, Barbra had achieved the pinnacle of success in everything she had attempted. Yet there was still one area she had not entered, one goal she hadn't yet fulfilled. That goal was to become a movie star.

Streisand in "Color Me Barbra." By 1966, she had conquered both stage and television.

On a Clear Day

arbra's last performance as Fanny Brice on the Broadway stage was in December 1965. It would take almost two and a half years for the movie version to hit America and make Streisand the country's biggest female star.

Ray Stark wanted to make Barbra's introduction to Hollywood a memorable one. He and his wife, Fran, planned to make a splash by hosting a party to end all parties, and the guest list was a who's who of Hollywood: Steve McQueen, John Wayne, Marlon Brando, Jimmy Stewart, Cary Grant, and Natalie Wood were among those who were invited. Fresh from New York and put on display for actors she had admired since her childhood, Barbra was understandably nervous. "Everybody who was anybody was invited to that thing," said one attendee. "Everybody had been in business with each other or in bed with each other. And here Barbra was, and she didn't know anybody." It was a disaster.

After agonizing over what clothes to wear and about her looks, Barbra arrived ninety minutes late. Her first words to Stark upon arriving were reportedly, "What's the idea of starting me off in this terrible lighting?" Purportedly intimidated by the sheer volume of Hollywood at the party, she shunned the guests, instead hiding in the mansion's library. The next day, the gossip about Barbra's snubbing the guests was all over Hollywood. "I was frightened," she said later of the event. "I was never a gregarious kind of person. I was always shy." Nevertheless, she repeated her mistake at another party for Carol Burnett at Rock Hudson's house. When she arrived she was greeted by journalists and photographers covering the event. "I didn't know people invited photographers to parties in their own homes," she said later. After a brief chat with the host and the guest of honor, Barbra and Elliot went to a drive-in and ate hamburgers. Her later comments to the press calling the locals "self-centered" and "boring" did nothing to endear her to the Hollywood establishment. At the very beginning, Barbra set herself up for criticism from her peers, which would haunt her for the rest of her Hollywood career.

Despite her poor relations with her new peer group, Barbra had done something that none of them had. By the time she hit Hollywood, she had, in addition to her role in *Funny Girl*, signed contracts with two other studios for big-budget musicals, *Hello, Dolly!* and *On a Clear Day You Can See Forever*, without ever having appeared on film. Stark, who had signed her to star in *Funny Girl*, initially had trouble landing a studio

Barbra as Fanny Brice in the movie version of Funny Girl. Before the film's release, she had already signed to star in two more films.

deal for the film, mostly because of Barbra's inexperience. Studios were wary of theatrical stars; many had not made a successful crossover to film stardom. Stark, however, was adamant: "I just felt she was too much a part of Fanny and Fanny was too much a part of Barbra to have it go to someone else." Columbia Pictures eventually required that she do a screen test for the picture. The film's choreographer, Herb Ross explained, "Once we saw her on the screen.... we knew that she was able to project on film as well as she projected on stage. In fact, the medium

was even more flattering to her." Ross himself was surprised at how fabulous Barbra looked on camera: "Onscreen she looked [like] a miracle." William Wyler, the legendary director of *Ben Hur*, *Wuthering Heights*, and *Roman Holiday*, was signed to direct the film, and he insisted that Ross be hired to direct and choreograph the musical numbers. All that was left was to find the leading man.

Columbia had under contract perhaps the country's sexiest leading man in Omar Sharif. His stunning performance in *Doctor Zhivago*

In a scene from Funny Girl with Omar Shariff as Nick Arnstein. Their pairing caused an international uproar.

along with his continental charm made him an easy choice for director Wyler. But Sharif was an Egyptian and Barbra a Jew, and the pairing of the two could have been jeopardized by the outbreak of the Six Day War. Instead, Stark capitalized on the Arab-Israeli conflict, playing up the couple in the international press. While the publicity was enormous, outraged Arabs con-

demned the two, and Barbra's films have never played in an Arab country since.

The film production, international controversy, and the demands of caring for her newborn baby apparently had little effect on Barbra's drive. On June 17, 1967, Barbra gave a free performance in New York's Central Park for an estimated 135,000 people, the largest audience

Thank you, New York—Barbra at her free concert in Central Park. She feared for her life while onstage.

for any performance there. The concert was taped and aired as a CBS television special, but during the entire evening, because of the controversy over her and Sharif's casting in *Funny Girl* and because of some pro-Israel statements she had recently made to the press, Barbra feared for her life. There was no incident, however and the concert was a rousing success, portrayed by the press as a thank-you to her fellow New Yorkers. In addition, the ensuing hour-long television special of the event was both a critical and ratings success.

During the making of *Funny Girl* Barbra's reputation for being a difficult star was reinforced. William Wyler had made more than sixty movies, had won eight Academy Awards, and was respected as a master in the Hollywood community. Nevertheless, Barbra had no problem confronting him when she found herself in disagreement with him over a scene. "Here was this young whippersnapper telling a very noted director how to do his job," one crew member later related. Yet Wyler, who had previously worked with other demanding actresses such as Bette Davis, was hardly the type to be run over by a young neophyte. "She was a bit obstreperous in the beginning, but things were ironed out when she discovered some of us knew what we were doing," he said. "Sometimes, she would argue for her way. If I was set on my way, that's the way we did it. She was not difficult in that sense. She was very cooperative." Besides her run-ins with the director, Barbra's insistence on doing her own makeup and wig design made her few friends in those departments. "What I saw her do to other people angered me so much that I couldn't tolerate her," one crew member said. But Barbra's most intense interest was in how she was being photographed. There have been conflicting accounts of her relationship with

director of photography Harry Stradling; some recount Stradling being furious with the young star for her incessant suggestions, while others tell of a patient older man schooling Barbra in how the photography process worked.

The most persistent and undeniable gossip about the production was of Barbra's affair with Omar Sharif. While Elliot Gould was in New York filming *The Night They Raided Minsky's*, Sharif and Barbra, according to Sharif, "led the very simple life of people in love." They were seen together first at a fashion show, then nuzzling together at a Hollywood restaurant. Confronted with the story by a gossip columnist, Gould was enraged: "I'm a very secure person, but as a man I have certain reactions." When the filming ended, so did the affair. Some say that Barbra broke it off in deference to her husband while others say on-set romances were standard procedure for Sharif. Nonetheless Barbra went home to New York and to her husband. Her next leading man would be much more problematic.

Hello, Dolly!, which was based on Thornton Wilder's play *The Matchmaker*, had originally been written as a Broadway musical showcase for Ethel Merman, but she rejected the part. Instead, Carol Channing made the show a smash on Broadway. So it was understandable that a few

Barbra and Omar
clown for the camera
on the set of Funny
Girl. Shariff had
flings with many of
his leading ladies.

hackles were raised when Barbra, not yet twenty-seven, was cast as Dolly Levi, a woman of "uncertain age." Nevertheless, Columbia hired no less than silver screen legend Gene Kelly to direct the picture and the wonderful character actor Walter Matthau to star as Horace Vandergelder, Dolly's love interest. It was not a match made in heaven.

Matthau was an old pro who respected Kelly's career and his accomplishments and had previously worked with Kelly on *A Guide for the Married Man*. He was also a no-nonsense actor who didn't appreciate the constant "suggestions" that Barbra offered to the director. Rumors also flew that Sidney Chaplin had already poisoned

*Right: With direc-
tor Gene Kelly on
the Hello, Dolly!
set.*

*Far right: Barbra
with Jason on the
Hello, Dolly! set.
Barbra would often
bring her young son
with her when she
was filming.*

Matthau's mind with horror stories of working with Streisand on *Funny Girl*. In fact, their first meeting had occurred three years earlier, when Matthau had approached her backstage at a Broadway play they were both attending and said, "You must be Barbara Harris. You ought to get that nose fixed." The relationship went downhill from there.

The big blowup came during filming in New York. Irate that Barbra was constantly giving Kelly suggestions on how he should play his role, Matthau erupted. "Stop directing the fucking picture!" he bellowed. Name calling fol-

lowed with Barbra calling Matthau "Old sewer mouth." "Nobody in this company likes you," Matthau responded, sending a sobbing Barbra back to her dressing room. "I found it a most unpleasant picture to work on and, as most of my scenes were with her, extremely distasteful," Matthau would later recall. With a great deal of relief to all concerned, the production wrapped in September 1968, as Barbra's career was about to soar to a whole new level.

On September 18, *Funny Girl* premiered at the Criterion Theater in New York. The film itself received mixed reviews, but not Barbra. Her per-

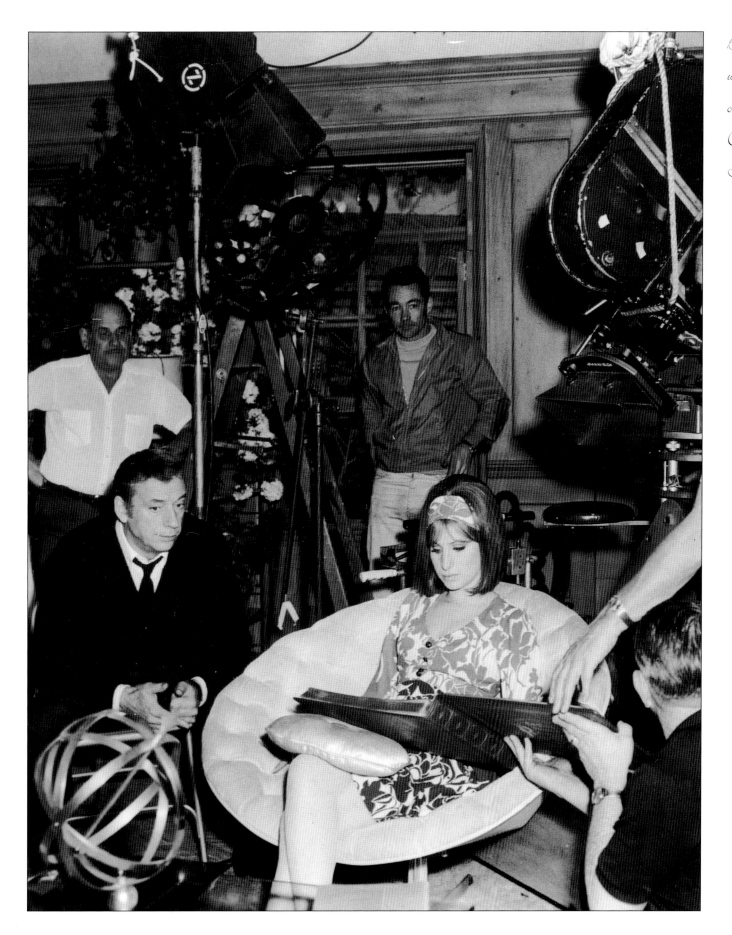

Barbra rehearses with Yves Montand on the set of On a Clear Day You Can See Forever.

ing her appear aloof. Her choice of denim overalls in the rhinestone capital of the world did not help her stage presence at all. *The Los Angeles Times* wrote, "Miss Streisand's appearance was a curious, cold, and intensely disappointing eighty minutes' worth." Barbra cried in her dressing room. The next night she went to see Peggy Lee, who was performing at another casino. Lee had the Vegas audience down cold and played them like a fiddle. Barbra was so impressed with her performance that she made changes in her own show, and the audiences came around. By the time the *Times* came around to see her show again, "It was a concert to remember."

Apparently Barbra ironed the wrinkles out of the International's concert hall, as none other than Elvis Presley was booked to follow her. He even saw Barbra's second to last performance. His visit to her backstage is the stuff of showbiz legend, although no one really knows what the two said. Rumors circulated that he disparaged Elliot Gould. One report even has the King down on his knees, painting Barbra's toenails. There are also reports that the two spent the night together. Whatever the case, Elvis was inspired. His performance at the International and the subsequent television special are collectively considered one of the greatest showbiz comebacks in history.

Barbra's recording career had stalled after the release of the *Funny Girl* film soundtrack. The material she had been performing up to that point was all from another era and she felt that in the "Age of Aquarius" she should try a more contemporary sound. The result was *What About Today?*, an album consisting of songs by contemporary artists like the Beatles and Buffy St. Marie. Her choice of material, however, did not pan out. *What About Today?* peaked at number thirty-one on the *Billboard* charts.

Barbra's next picture, *The Owl and the Pussycat*, began filming in October 1969. It was notable because it was Barbra's first nonmusical. Barbra was determined to show herself as a true actress, not just a singer who performed in movie-musicals. *The Owl and the Pussycat* was also a riotous comedy, with Streisand playing a streetwise hooker who falls for a nerdy writer who works in a bookstore. Directed by Herb Ross and costarring the handsome young actor George Segal, who had wowed audiences in his dramatic performance in *Who's Afraid of Virginia Woolf?*, *The Owl and the Pussycat* also featured Barbra's only nude scene, as she drops her robe before climbing into bed with her costar. Perhaps Barbra saw it as a radical way to distance herself from the past and jump into a new, more modern

A scene from The Owl and the Pussycat, in which the costumes were as outlandish as the story.

*Barbra's intense
film and television
schedules made her
live performances a
rare commodity.*

persona. In the end, however, she could not over-come her shyness and demanded that the nudity be removed.

Hello, Dolly! premiered in December 1969. The evening was marred by the frenzy of fans waiting at the Rivoli Theater in New York. When Barbra's limo arrived, the fans turned into a mob and a riot broke out outside her car. They pounded on the hood and screamed her name. Barbra sat in the back horrified, afraid to get out until almost half an hour later when police had moved the crowd back. Security then formed a barrier, standing around the star as she made her way through the mob. It was superstardom at its ugliest.

Since *Funny Girl* had been so successful, every-one assumed that *Hello, Dolly!* would be a surefire hit. The reviews were overwhelmingly favorable, and initially, it seemed headed for box-office mil-lions. It received seven Oscar nominations the fol-lowing February, including Best Picture (though, notably, not Best Actress). But then business went sour and attendances waned. The huge budget of the picture made it essential that the film be a huge hit, or it would lose money. And lose money it did, grossing less than $40 million, far less than needed to break even. Film historians have pointed to *Hello, Dolly!* as the end of the Hollywood musical.

Barbra arrives at the premier of Hello, Dolly! in 1969.

The
Way
We
Were

W

hen 1970 began, Barbra was caught in a curious dilemma. On one hand she was an acknowledged superstar who had two movies out, one "in the can," and one about to begin production. On the other hand, she was famous for a genre that had dropped out of sight—the Hollywood musical. She was in danger of becoming a dinosaur before her thirtieth birthday because she could not connect with a younger, hipper audience.

Barbra spent much of the month of January 1970 in Canada, attending the Centennial of Manitoba's arts festival. This would have been noticed only as an odd appearance for the Brooklyn-born superstar were it not for the real reason for her visit: her escort was the dazzling young Canadian prime minister, Pierre Trudeau. Barbra had met Trudeau in London when she had been there for the premiere of *Funny Girl*. But that had been the old, musical-theater, married Barbra. This was the new, glamorous, hip Barbra, and the relationship was taking the country by storm. She even attended a session of Parliament, where the two openly flirted. Speculations about marriage and "First Lady Barbra" appeared in the press. But the relationship between a superstar in the prime of her career and a politician who would obviously

demand most of his wife's time was doomed. Ironically, Barbra, who had done her share of philandering, was the victim of the same when she discovered Trudeau was also seeing one Margaret Sinclair, whom he married in 1971.

On a Clear Day You Can See Forever opened in June 1970 to little fanfare. The wilting of *Hello, Dolly!* had convinced the studios that the old-fashioned Broadway musical was dead. Although *On a Clear Day* brought in only $13.4 million, the modest budget allowed the movie to break even. The movie was decidedly behind the times and decidedly square especially when held up against such contemporary films as *MASH*, *Bob & Carol & Ted & Alice*, and *Getting Straight*, all of which starred none other than

*Barbra tries her
wings in a scene for
On a Clear Day
You Can See
Forever. The film
was a modest success,
but by its release,
Hollywood was
already moving away
from musicals.*

Elliot Gould. In fact, Gould's success prompted the National Association of Theater Owners to name him their "Star of the Year." *Time* magazine featured him on its cover, with the banner headline "Star for an Uptight Age."

It was precisely that uptight image that Barbra again tried to shed when she put together her next album. Unbowed by the poor sales of *What About Today?* she turned to producer Richard Perry, who was ecstatic about the prospect of

helping her make the transition to modern pop music. "Here was the greatest vocal instrument of our generation," he said, "not at all relating to popular contemporary music."

Discarding a collection of songs she had recorded earlier in the year entitled *The Singer*, she took up the newer material with zest. She recorded songs by some of the best contemporary songwriters, including Joni Mitchell and Randy Newman, and most notably sang Laura

Nyro's composition "Stoney End, Stoney End," which had previously been recorded by various other artists, including *Mod Squad* sex symbol Peggy Lipton. Columbia Records president Clive Davis believed he had a hit, however, and he was eventually proven right when the song reached number six on the charts. Columbia followed up the single with the release of an album of the same name, which won Streisand

terrific reviews and landed in the top ten of *Billboard's* charts. Barbra was once again contemporary, and she was enormously successful at the same time.

Barbra's first role in a nonmusical film, *The Owl and the Pussycat*, opened in November 1970 with a decidedly racy advertising campaign. It received favorable reviews and became one of the most successful films of the year.

Streisand loosens up while preforming at Las Vegas' Riviera in 1970.

Barbra was again playing Las Vegas at the end of 1970, first at the Riviera and then at the Hilton. The lessons she learned from her appearance at the International were paying off; she was much more comfortable with the Vegas audience—but maybe too comfortable. She had developed a sketch in which she made light of her nervousness in front of a paying crowd. As it went in the sketch, she would smoke marijuana to try to calm down. She produced a prop joint and pretended to get stoned. On the final night of her performance, she took her act to the limit. According to Barbra, "I started lighting live joints, passing them around to the band....it was great." The show rapidly deteriorated as Barbra got more and more stoned, until it dissolved into a rambling monologue. One year later, she would again perform in Vegas at the Las Vegas Hilton. It would be her last performance for the general public for fifteen years.

Meanwhile, Elliot Gould was going insane. At least that's what Warner Bros. thought when his exploits leaked to them. Gould's use of drugs was undermining his career. His erratic behavior on the set of his latest film, *A Glimpse of Tiger*, caused the studio to shut down the production and sue the actor. During the shoot he fired director Anthony Harvey, and threatened bodily harm to his costar Kim Darby and the director. The studio put together a file with details of Gould's erratic behavior for a group of psychiatrists, who pronounced him insane. Warner Bros. used the doctor's findings to collect their production costs from the insurers of the movie. Gould was later quite candid about this period in his life: "Even Elvis Presley, who'd said he was an admirer of mine, sat down in front of me, a gold .45 in his belt, and told me, 'You're crazy.'" But as things tend to work out in Hollywood, Gould's trouble would lead to a triumph for Barbra.

Concerned about Gould's welfare, Barbra approached Warner Bros. and asked if there was anything she could do to prevent the studio from suing the actor. They suggested that she star in the aborted production, with the starring role rewritten for a woman. They even had a new, hip young director to work with her by the name of Peter Bogdanovich, who created a sensation with his film *The Last Picture Show*. Barbra agreed, providing that she star opposite her new boyfriend, Ryan O'Neal. The studio assented, but there was one problem. Bogdanovich didn't want to do *A Glimpse of Tiger*. He wanted to do an old-fashioned comedy like they used to do in the thirties and forties.

Ryan O'Neal came to America's attention playing Rodney Harrington on the soap opera *Peyton Place*. But it was his leading role in *Love Story*, costarring Ali McGraw, that made him a star. The ex-boxer was nominated for an Academy Award for his performance. Barbra and he had met at a dinner party and carried on a not-too-subtle affair while O'Neal remained married to actress Leigh Taylor-Young. Then two things happened that allowed the pair to go public. Taylor-Young and O'Neal announced their separation and, in Santo Domingo, Dominican Republic, Elliot Gould officially divorced Barbra. After that Barbra and Ryan were a regular couple at parties and public events—and now they were to costar.

Because of *Stoney End's* success, Columbia was anxious for Barbra to put out another album featuring contemporary material. With tunes by James Taylor, Michel Legrand, Marilyn and Alan Bergman, and John Lennon, Barbra's next album, *Barbra Joan Streisand*, was tremendously popular with her fans. But despite its sales success—it was certified gold—it would be the last contemporary album she would put out for three years.

On August 16, 1971, Barbra began work on her next film, *What's Up, Doc?*, but with trepidation. Despite director Peter Bogdanovich's success with *The Last Picture Show* and a script by David Newman and Robert Benton, whose last effort, *Bonnie and Clyde*, was nominated for an Academy Award, Barbra was convinced she was making a bomb. Bogdanovich kept trying to reassure her: "It'll play funny, Barbra, you'll see. Trust me." And trust him she did. Barbra gave up her hard-fought-for creative control over script and casting to do the film. Bogdanovich was very much a controlling personality. "She tried to direct me, but we put a stop to that real quick," he later said. The fast pace of the film and the slapstick elements took its toll; O'Neal suffered a serious back injury during the shooting of the climatic chase scene.

By the end of the filming Barbra and Ryan had split up, largely over the fact that O'Neal and Peggy Lipton were having a fling. Barbra was soon seen on the social circuit with superstar actor Steve McQueen. Yet there was still a soft spot in Barbra's heart for O'Neal. She visited him several times in the hospital after he had surgery to remove two disks from his spine. "He was lying in bed, and you know, he has that terribly irresistible little-boy quality about him. I have that terrible Brooklyn Jewish need to mother. Maybe that's why we get along so well," she recalled later.

Barbra with her co-
star and boyfriend
Ryan O'Neal on the
set of What's Up,
Doc?

The Way
We Were
61

Barbra was so convinced that *What's Up, Doc?* was going to be a failure that she sold her share in the film back to the studio. "I was embarrassed to do that film," she said. "It was a disappointing experience." For one of the few times in her life, Barbra was wrong about one of her pictures. When *What's Up, Doc?* was released the following March, it drew rave reviews and grossed more than $50 million at the box office.

Barbra turned thirty in 1972 and her maturing also brought on a keen interest in politics and social issues other than her passion for Jewish issues and support for Israel. The beginning of the decade also marked the beginning of America's women's movement, and Barbra was finding herself at odds with her professional career and her desire to be a good parent. Believing her reputation of being difficult was a result of blatant sexism, she told one reporter, "I had ideas, and I expressed them. But because I was a woman, I was disregarded. There is this prejudice against actresses. They're supposed to look pretty and read their lines, then shut up and go home." At the same time, she could not identify with women's groups who advocated a complete abandonment of traditional women's roles. Barbra continued, "Many women today are in conflict with their role in society. They feel they should be allowed to do more, yet they still have that primal urge of mothering. Most of all, a woman should be allowed to do what she wants."

It seemed natural for Barbra to combine her clout as a professional with her views on women's roles when her company, Barwood Films, produced her next film, *Up the Sandbox*. In 1969, in her quest for more control over what movies she made, Barbra formed First Artists along with Paul Newman and Sidney Poitier. The company was designed to produce each actor's pictures and allow them creative control of the finished product. Steve McQueen and Dustin Hoffman would later join the company. *Up the Sandbox* would be Barbra's first picture distributed by First Artists.

In *Up the Sandbox*, Barbra played Margaret Reynolds, a young housewife who questions her role as a mother as she contemplates whether or not to have a second child. Her thoughts are played out in a series of vignettes in which she alternately is attacked by African tribeswomen, blows up the Statue of Liberty, and discovers that Fidel Castro is really a woman. In the end, she is convinced that her role as a mother is worthwhile.

Before beginning principal photography for *Up the Sandbox*, Barbra agreed to perform at the Los Angeles Forum in a concert fund-raiser for presidential candidate George McGovern. Following Carole King and James Taylor, Barbra performed to a packed house that featured stars in the seats and actually working the floor as ushers. Goldie Hawn and Jack Nicholson were among the volunteers. Her encore of "People" brought down the house, and the benefit raised more than $300,000 for McGovern's ill-fated campaign.

Up the Sandbox suffered from the inability of the filmmakers to successfully translate the original novel, by Anne Richardson Roiphe, into a cohesive movie storyline. "All the drama was in the fantasies, which didn't work because you knew it wasn't really happening," the film's director, Irvin Kershner, would later lament. The film was notable for the sequences that were filmed in Africa, but despite Barbra's rare feat of actively promoting the film, *Up the Sandbox* would turn out to be a critical and box-office flop. Perhaps it was a victim of its own political message, or it may have suffered from an advertising campaign that made it out to be a madcap farce like *The Owl and the Pussycat*. Either way, Barbra's first effort at producing was a failure.

"God, if only we could convince Redford!" Barbra exclaimed. Ray Stark had signed Barbra to star in his next picture, *The Way We Were*, which chronicled the ill-fated marriage of a communist activist to a WASPy hunk during the 1930s. Stark and Barbra had bounced the names of almost every leading man in Hollywood back and forth, but they always came back to Robert Redford. The young actor had a string of hits and was one of Hollywood's leading heartthrobs. There was much speculation that Barbra wanted to work with Redford more because of her personal infatuation with the actor than with any professional desire to work with him. Stark had worked with Redford before, in *This Property Is Condemned*, which was directed by Sidney Pollack. Pollack had also recently directed Redford in *Jeremiah Johnson*, so Stark's strategy was to get Pollack so that Redford would also come.

Redford was mainly concerned that while Streisand's character, Katie Morosky, was a passionate activist, the character they wanted him to play, Hubbel Gardiner, lacked any goal or drive altogether. "Who is this guy?" he complained to Pollack. "He's just an object. A nothing." Pollack hired respected screenwriters Alvin Sargent and

Barbra as Margaret Reynolds in Up the Sandbox, her first movie as star and producer.

The Way We Were with Robert Redford. Barbra was completely infatuated with her handsome co-star.

David Rayfiel to do rewrites on the original script by Arthur Laurents. Based on his relationship with Pollack and his faith in the writers, Redford finally signed on.

During the production of *The Way We Were*, it was obvious that Barbra was in awe of her leading man. She admired Redford's commitment to his craft and his workmanlike approach to his character. However, their acting methods could not have been more different. While Barbra was exacting and controlling, Redford was more spontaneous, often seeking new ways

to approach the scene on the spot. Despite his personal affection for Barbra, Redford found the making of the film "like doing overtime at Dachau." Meanwhile, Pollack was constantly under pressure from Stark and Columbia (which was having financial difficulties) to keep the production costs down and finish on time. And there was constant rewriting going on while the film was in production. Add the fact that neither Pollack nor Redford got along with Ray Stark and it is not surprising that neither remember the making of the film with any fondness. "Truthfully, nobody had any faith in the picture," Pollack later said.

Pollack hired Barbra's old rehearsal pianist from her Broadway days in *Funny Girl*, Marvin Hamlisch, to score *The Way We Were* and write the title song, with lyrics by Marilyn and Alan Bergman. Barbra didn't like the song, which was designed to go over the closing credits of the movie. "I had to beg her to sing it," the composer later said. Barbra asked Hamlisch to write another tune, which he grudgingly did. Pollack suggested they play both versions against the end of the movie and vote on which worked best. Hamlisch's original version won out. The soundtrack's title single became a number one hit and was named *Billboard's* top pop single of the year. It was Barbra's first hit single in three years.

The Way We Were opened in October 1973, and although the reviews were decidedly mixed, it was an outright smash. Her onscreen chemistry with Redford and the film's tearjerker ending proved irresistible to a public that hadn't seen this kind of film since *Love Story*. Barbra was again nominated for an Academy Award, while Redford was nominated for his role in another of that year's smashes, *The Sting*.

Joanne Woodward, Marsha Mason, Ellen Burstyn, and Glenda Jackson were Barbra's competition for that year's Oscar—competition not nearly as strong as she had faced when nominated for *Funny Girl*. Barbra was confident about her performance. "I felt it was the best of those five for the year," she said. "I felt I deserved the award." However, it was not to be. In a surprise vote, Jackson won out for her performance in *A Touch of Class*. Believing, like everyone else, that she had little chance of winning, the actress didn't even attend the ceremony. Many people, including Barbra herself, believed that she lost out on the award because her Hollywood peers disliked her. True or not, the snubbing Barbra endured that night would be repeated throughout her career.

The end of 1973 also marked the end of Barbra's work on network television specials. Coinciding with the release of *The Way We Were*, "Barbra Streisand and Other Musical Instruments" aired on the CBS network on November 2, 1973, with decidedly disappointing results. Aside from a stirring duet with Ray Charles on his composition "Cryin' Time," the reviewers panned her performance. Television viewers did not tune in. Since her concert in Central Park, Barbra had appeared only four times on television. It would be fifteen years before she would again perform on the small screen.

FIVE

Evergreen

J on Peters was already a millionaire when Barbra first met him in the summer of 1973. The twenty-eight-year-old had a past that seemed unlikely for a hairdresser to the stars. A juvenile delinquent who never went to high school, Peters had already established a chain of hair salons, married twice (the second time to actress Lesley Ann Warren), and become a minor celebrity in his own right when Barbra called him to create a new look for her next film, *For Pete's Sake*. Following his divorce from Warren, Peters was a notorious playboy and his lifestyle was rumored to be the model for the Warren Beatty movie *Shampoo*.

When Peters showed up at Barbra's house in Los Angeles, it was love at first sight. "She was vulnerable and beautiful. Immediately the chemistry started working between us," Peters has said of that initial meeting. Barbra was taken aback at the way Peters treated her. He was not intimidated by her stardom and he was frank about his sexual attraction for her. "He just made me feel very young and beautiful, and he said, 'The public should see this side of you— the sexy side, your legs, your ass, your breasts'," Barbra later recalled. Their attraction for each other would simmer, for Barbra soon left Los Angeles for New York to begin shooting *For Pete's Sake*.

For Pete's Sake was an attempt to recapture the success and zany comedy of *What's Up, Doc?*, and was also her manager Marty Erlichman's first shot at producing a movie. Directed by Peter Yates and costarring Michael Sarrazin and Estelle Parsons, *For Pete's Sake* was a chore for Barbra. For one, it brought her back to Brooklyn, which she now hated as it symbolized her troubled background, and it kept her away from Peters.

Barbra had turned down many starring roles in the previous years, among them the lead in *Cabaret*, which won Liza Minnelli an Oscar, and *They Shoot Horses, Don't They?*, which Jane Fonda eventually starred in. The success of *The Way We Were* showed that Barbra had an eye for good material. Her choice to star in *For Pete's Sake* clouded that reputation. An attempt to repeat the slapstick silliness that was so successful in *What's Up, Doc?*, *For Pete's Sake* was nevertheless an odd choice for Barbra—unusual in that it wallowed in comic devices that could be perceived as insensitive at best, callous at worst. Barbra played a Brooklyn housewife named Henry who, in order to bolster her husband's failures as a businessman, borrows money from the Mafia, becomes a hooker, and rustles cattle. The picture also contains derogatory references

Page 66: Barbra once again played the character Fanny Brice in Funny Lady.

Page 67: Despite Barbra's apprehensions about doing a musical, Funny Lady was a massive success.

to gays, which seems incomprehensible considering her political activism and her legions of gay fans. Perhaps her experience with *Up the Sandbox*—perceived as trying too hard to make a point—led her to star in this Peter Yates film. *For Pete's Sake* was panned by just about every major critic when it opened in June 1974. Luckily for Barbra, her mind was on other things.

The Hollywood press was seeing something it couldn't believe. Barbra Streisand was acting like a schoolgirl. She was in love with her hairdresser, who was three years younger than she. Since legally separating from his second wife, Jon Peters was seen everywhere with Barbra. Naturally the cynical press made much of Peters' being a hairdresser, but this particular hairdresser was pulling in over six figures a

As Henry the Brooklyn housewife in For Pete's Sake. The film was an ill-conceived attempt to repeat the success of What's Up, Doc?

week from his three fabulously successful salons. Any snickers over Peters' profession being something less than macho were silenced by his brawling background. In fact, many credit Peters with getting Barbra out of Tinseltown to travel on skiing and camping vacations. She spent time in her garden and took up eating health foods. "I don't need to work anymore to feed my ego," she said. "I get all the ego nourishment I need from him."

"There is no way I will do this movie!" Barbra roared at Ray Stark. Nevertheless, Barbra signed on to do the sequel to *Funny Girl* for the producer. The only possible answer to speculation as to why the actress would return to a genre that she had successfully left years before had to do with Liza Minnelli. Liza won the Tony Award the year after Barbra lost it for *Funny Girl* and had become a quick success in films, being nominated for an Oscar for her role in *The Sterile Cuckoo*. She also won an Emmy for her television special, "Liza with a Z," and won an Oscar for Best Actress for her spectacular performance in *Cabaret*. So perhaps it was Minnelli's success that prompted Barbra to re-enter the musical genre. Rehearsals for *Funny Lady* began the morning after Barbra lost out to Glenda Jackson at the Academy Awards for *The Way We Were*.

The filming of *Funny Lady* was like old times; Barbra and Ray Stark bickered continually throughout the production. Of course, trouble continued when costar James Caan broke his finger during the production when he participated in a Palm Springs rodeo. Stark was furious about the extra time needed to shoot around the cast Caan had to wear, and even forced Caan to cut it off during close-ups featuring the two stars. The casting of Caan, the tall, handsome costar of *The Godfather*, as Billy Rose, who in actuality was five feet tall in elevator shoes, rather than a more diminutive actor such as Al Pacino or Robert Blake, was defended by Barbra this way: "It comes down to whom the audience wants me to kiss. Robert Blake, no. James Caan, yes." Barbra was as exacting as ever. Cinematographer Vilmos Zsigmond was fired after only two days on the set. Apparently unhappy with the future Oscar winner's more realistic lighting, Barbra had him replaced with veteran James Wong Howe. Howe had been in the business since the dawn of the talkies, and *Funny Lady* was the last film he would photograph; he died two years later. Omar Sharif, whose star was on the wane, agreed to reprise his role as Nicky Arnstein in a few brief scenes.

One production highlight on *Funny Lady* was when Fanny Brice goes up in a 1930s biplane. Insisting that audiences would recognize a double in the plane, director Herbert Ross convinced the reluctant star to go up in the open plane herself. After taking off from the Santa Monica Airport and circling the cameras a few times, the plane was forced to delay its landing due to traffic congestion at the airport. When the plane finally touched down, Barbra was panic-stricken. She believed that the shot was all a part of an elaborate plot to kidnap her. Somehow, Ross convinced her to go up and do the shot again.

Jon Peters visited the set often. The press had it that Jon was keeping an eye on Caan and Sharif, but Jon was actually trying to learn about the business of filmmaking. In director

Barbra and co-star James Cann on the set of Funny Lady in 1975. Barbra's return to the big Hollywood musical was also a return to the character that made her a star.

Herb Ross' view, however, it distracted Barbra. "She was in love at the time, and she didn't seem to want to make the picture or play the part. It was a movie that was made virtually without her. She simply wasn't there in terms of commitment, and one of her greatest qualities is to make a thousand percent commitment." Barbra later agreed somewhat: "When I had a lack in my private life I cared more about my work." Despite this seeming lack of commitment, *Funny Lady* completed production in July 1974. Her next project would be for another producer: Jon Peters.

Before the production of *Funny Lady*, Barbra had begun work on her new album, *Butterfly*. Peters was producing the album and his inexperience slowed the project. The couple encountered resistance and ridicule from the outset. Columbia was unhappy with everything about the concept, from the selection of songs to the way they were recorded. After hearing several of the proposed cuts for the album, they sent out veteran record engineer Al Schmitt, who lasted just a few days. His comments to a reporter were scathing. "Peters is a nice guy, but he's not a record producer," he told a reporter. "Essentially, Peters wanted all the money and I'd be doing all the work.... Streisand has this tremendous thing

of knowing exactly what's right for her. But now, it seems that's gone out the window. She's never let anyone direct her career this way." The critics were also caustic: *Butterfly* was called "one of the worst albums made by a major talent" and "an all-time recording low"; David Bowie, whose song "Life on Mars" she covered, said of her version, "Sorry, Barb, but it was atrocious." Nonetheless, *Butterfly* went to number thirteen on the *Billboard* charts and went gold after just three months.

Novelist and screenwriter John Gregory Dunne and his wife, writer Joan Didion, were on their way to the Honolulu Airport when Dunne blurted out, "James Taylor and Carly Simon in a rock remake of *A Star Is Born*." The writers took their idea to Warner Bros., who owned the twice-retold story of the movie legend on the spiral downward and his true love who was on the opposite path. The saga was apparently too close to reality for husband and wife Taylor and Simon, who declined the parts. After several rewrites, screenwriters, producers, and directors had come and gone, and the project, now titled *Rainbow Road*, ended up in the hands of Jon Peters.

"The world is waiting to see Barbra's and my story!" Peters said in the first meeting that he and Barbra had with Dunne and Didion, now back on the story due to Barbra's interest. Barbra was worried, however, that the male lead was too strong; she wanted her part beefed up and, above all, "more love story." Peters and Streisand were not happy with the drafts that the writers turned in. They were also aggressively pushing Warner Bros. to assign the rights to the movie to Barbra's First Artists production company and to have Peters produce the film.

Hollywood exists on chutzpah and no one had more than Peters. Notwithstanding the fact that he had never done anything in the film business (except an appearance in *The Ten Commandments* when he was a child), he and Barbra were convinced that he was the only one who could do the movie justice. After all, the movie was about them. "It touches on the facts of my life," Peters said, "the street fighter and overachiever. The macho thing is very much me. I fought for what I believed in and was not above using violence." Peters' influence over Barbra was overwhelming. Jerry Schatzberg, who was to direct the movie and actually introduced Peters to the script, later related, "His influence over her was very strong.... He was like Rasputin or Svengali with her." Soon the production process was littered with writers whose take on the material was not to the

couple's liking. Didion and Dunne were forced out, left with a handsome severance pay. Now Kris Kristofferson, the songwriter who had made a name for himself in such pictures as *Cisco Pike*, *Blume in Love*, and *Alice Doesn't Live Here Anymore* and who had been attached to the project when Peters got a hold of it, was threatening to walk. Schatzberg received a call from Barbra: "What do you think of Jon playing opposite to me?" Schatzberg left the picture.

Funny Lady opened on March 9, 1975, and the critics heaped praise on Barbra's performance. One film critic even suggested that her artistry was such that she should be nominated for a Nobel Prize. Barbra promoted the picture's opening with a benefit performance for the Special Olympics at the Kennedy Center in Washington, D.C. The performance, billed as "Funny Girl to Funny Lady," was broadcast live over ABC. Despite Barbra's lack of enthusiasm during production, the film was a hit, grossing $48 million.

The cover of the March 1975 issue of *New Times* featured a rendering of a bald Barbra Streisand with the title "A Star Is Shorn." The article referred to the *A Star is Born* project as "Hollywood's biggest joke" and portrayed Barbra and Jon as two rich kids out of control.

While this was certainly not the first time the two had been ridiculed in the press, it upset Peters, who had given the reporter his full cooperation for the story. Most notable in the article was the revelation that Peters now intended to direct *Rainbow Road*, which had been retitled *A Star Is Born*. "Directing is a thing I've done all my life! It's getting people to do what I want them to do!" the article quoted him as saying.

Barbra and Jon flew to Las Vegas in April to talk to Elvis Presley, their first choice to play John Normand Howard. They were disgusted with the man they had come to see. "He was so fat he looked almost pregnant," Jon recalled. Although Presley was the perfect choice for the modern-day version of the Howard character—a legend on a rapid spiral downward—he was in no condition to actually play the part.

In the meantime, Jon and Barbra thought they had found the perfect writer in Frank Pierson. The fifty-year-old screenwriter was hot after his script for *Dog Day Afternoon* was made into a

Letting it all hang out with Kris Kristofferson in A Star Is Born. Despite their off-screen differences, the two stars made the movie a smash with their on-screen chemistry.

spellbinding film. Pierson agreed with Barbra that the story should be updated with the social changes that were taking place in the mid-seventies. However, Pierson had one condition for working on the film: that he direct it. Surprisingly, Barbra and Jon agreed, and *A Star Is Born* had its director.

As so much of the music for *A Star Is Born* would be filmed live, Barbra, Jon, and Pierson narrowed their choice of leading men down to Mick Jagger of the Rolling Stones and Kris Kristofferson. Barbra and Kris had dated briefly after her breakup with Elliot Gould. Her reasoning for considering Kris: "He's an actor. He's beautiful to look at. He can sing and play the guitar. And he's a Gentile, which seems to work with me—the Jew and the Gentile." Barbra was showing her knack of knowing what was good for her—in this case, the chemistry between the two stars would light up the screen and blow up on the set.

Finally there was the music. Barbra loved a song called "I Won't Last a Day Without You," which was penned by Paul Williams. "She called me on the phone, but evidently, I wasn't listening," Williams said. "She only wanted one song for the end of the picture.... What I had heard, however, and I don't know if it was my own grandiosity or what, was that she wanted me to

write all the songs for this movie." Perhaps admiring his perceived moxie at wanting to write all the movie's material, Jon and Barbra agreed, even giving him final control over the use of his music in the movie. "The only person who got any latitude with that," said Williams, "was Kris. I have so much respect for him. I mean, Kristofferson!" This was a one-sided fan club; Kristofferson was not a fan of Williams' music. At a meeting with the director, Jon, Barbra, and Williams, Kristofferson made it clear that he wanted to use his own music. Barbra felt that Kristofferson's country rock wasn't in tune with the Bruce Springsteen songs that were burning up the charts. When Jon agreed with her, Kris erupted: "Who shall I say says my music isn't rock—Barbra Streisand's hairdresser?" Then he stormed off. Williams took umbrage with Jon, saying that he didn't defend his music. This ended in a shouting match, with the tiny songwriter taking a swing at Peters before he stormed out. Meanwhile, principal photography was to begin in two weeks.

The highlight of *A Star Is Born* is a live concert filmed in front of a real audience. To entice an audience to Arizona's Sun Devil Stadium, the production engaged Peter Frampton and Santana to perform after the film performance.

To promote the film, members of the press were invited to an "official" press conference, after which the reporters lapped up the free food and drink provided for them while the actors returned to the stage for more rehearsal. What the performers didn't realize was that the sound technicians were also rehearsing, and that their conversations were being broadcast live to the feeding media. Kristofferson was infuriated by Barbra, who was trying to direct his performance. "Look, you're not doing what I tell you to do," Barbra shouted at him. "Listen to me when I talk to you, goddamm it!" "Fuck off!" Kristofferson retorted. "I'll be goddamned if I listen to anything more from you!" Then Jon entered the fray. "You owe my lady an apology," he shouted. "If I need any shit from you," Kristofferson yelled, "I'll squeeze your head."

The next day actual filming began in front of fifty thousand fans. The filming was slow and laborious, and the 100°F heat didn't help matters. The crowd began to chant, "No more filming, no more filming!" Barbra walked to the stage to calm the pandemonium, and proceeded to deliver the most unusual speech of her life. "We're going to do rock and roll today! And we're going to be in a movie! In our movie we're real. We fight, scream, yell, we talk dirty, we smoke grass! So, listen, what we're going to do now is meet my costar, Kris Kristofferson. A great performer. So when he comes on, I know you all love him anyway, but you have to love him even more, you know, so we won't have any problems. So, in the lingo of the movie, I say, all you motherfuckers have a great time." It worked. The crowd "performed" enthusiastically, and when it came time for Barbra to sing, the audience went wild. After singing "The Way We Were," she announced that she was going to sing a song she had written for the film. "I hope you like it. If you don't I'll be crushed." The song was "Evergreen."

Early in the production, Barbra had called Paul Williams and asked if he would put music to a tune that she had written on the guitar. One can imagine the uncomfortable prospect of listening to the very first writing effort of a major star—what if it was horrible? To Williams' surprise, he loved it. Agreeing to write the lyrics was the first thing he did on the production. Actually finishing it would be the last.

A *Star Is Born* received some of the most vicious reviews of Barbra's entire career. Critic Rex Reed wrote, "What the hell does Barbra Streisand know about directing and editing a movie? So many people have disowned this film

With her boyfriend and producer Jon Peters, backstage at the Golden Globe Awards in 1976.

that I don't even know who to blame. But I do blame a studio for giving $5.5 million to an actress and her boyfriend to finance their own ego trip." But when the movie opened on Christmas day in 1975, there were lines in front of every movie house in America. The film was a huge smash, grossing more than $150 million. It became Barbra's biggest movie to date, winning five Golden Globes for Best Picture, Actress, Actor, Song, and Score. The soundtrack went to

number one on the *Billboard* album charts and became the biggest-selling musical soundtrack. "Evergreen" went to number one on the singles charts and sold more than a million copies. And perhaps most important to Barbra, she won an Academy Award—not for acting, but for cowriting "Evergreen." Peters, who had feared the worst, was a huge success as a producer. "We planned on breaking up," he said, "but then the movie was a hit."

The Main Event

Gary Guthrie was heartsick. The Louisville, Kentucky, disc jockey was going through an amicable divorce in 1978 when he had an inspired idea. Neil Diamond had just released a song that he had written with Alan and Marilyn Bergman entitled "You Don't Bring Me Flowers." Barbra Streisand had also recorded the tune for her upcoming *Songbird* album. Guthrie spliced the two versions together to make a duet and presented the recording to his ex-wife as a gesture of his feelings. For a lark, the station played it on the air the next day. "All of a sudden, the phones started going bananas," Guthrie later said. Record stores all over the city were calling in asking where they could get the recording for the thousands of requests they were getting from their customers. Upon hearing this, executives at Columbia Records, for whom both Barbra and Diamond recorded, sent Guthrie and his station a cease-and-desist letter, then asked the two superstars into the studio to make an "official" duet. Ironically, Diamond and Barbra had both attended Erasmus Hall High School together and sang in the school choir, but they had never known each other. The duo sang the song unannounced at the 1980 Grammy Awards in Los Angeles. The song remains one of Barbra's most successful recordings, hitting number one on the *Billboard* singles charts within weeks of its release.

Songbird was preceded by the album, *Streisand Superman. Superman* featured Barbra on the cover in an outfit she appeared in briefly in *A Star Is Born*—skimpy shorts and a shirt with the Superman logo. She would later appear on the cover of *Playboy* magazine—which featured a rare and extensive interview—in the same outfit with the Playboy logo on the shirt. She was the first female movie star to appear on the magazine's cover since Marilyn Monroe some two decades earlier.

In the meantime, Jon Peters was trying to make a name for himself as a producer away from Barbra. His first movie after *A Star Is Born* was the thriller *The Eyes of Laura Mars*, starring Faye Dunaway. Barbra was involved, however, by singing "Prisoner" on the soundtrack. *The Eyes of Laura Mars* was a moderate success, although for Peters it certainly didn't live up to his first attempt. But the budding producer had another project in mind for Barbra, one that appealed to his love of the sport of boxing: a script entitled *Knockout*.

Knockout detailed the story of Hillary Kramer, a businesswoman swindled out of her money by her accountant. The only asset she has left is the

At the 1980 Grammy Awards with Neil Diamond. When the photographer, famed paparazzo Ron Galella asked for a photo, Barbra told him, "No focusing, take my good side."

contract of a has-been prize fighter. The desperate Kramer tries to force the fighter back into the ring to make her some money. The resulting "battle" of the sexes leads to love. Besides Peters, Barbra knew another boxing enthusiast who just happened to be a former boyfriend and costar.

Ryan O'Neal had come off a string of disappointing films and, given his past film success with Barbra, was eager to sign on. Barbra no doubt enjoyed the sparks between her current and former lovers on the set. Apparently O'Neal was getting his money's worth as well. "Ryan

As Cheryl Gibbons in All Night Long with Gene Hackman. The soap opera surrounding the making of the movie was more intriguing than the movie's plot.

anxious to see if she could team up with the group. The Bee Gees' principal writer and producer was the oldest brother of the group, Barry Gibb. Barry was a little hesitant about working for Barbra. "I was very nervous at first," he later said. "We all had heard the stories about how tough she is, and she is this enormous star. That's got to intimidate anyone." Barbra's producer, Charles Koppleman, sent Barry a few songs that Barbra was considering for her upcoming album, which Barry rejected. "I didn't think any of them had the little extra bit

that it takes to make a hit," he recalled. So the Gibb brothers wrote their own songs for her, including a duet, "Guilty," to be sung by Barbra and Barry. The resulting album named after that song was a huge hit. With a number one single, "Woman in Love," and two more songs in the top ten, the album itself reached number one status, selling more than ten million copies. It is still Barbra's best-selling album.

With two enormously successful films back-to-back and number one hits on the radio, everyone was surprised when the Hollywood trade papers announced that Barbra was replacing Lisa Eichhorn in the movie *All Night Long*. What was surprising was that Barbra was accepting second billing to Gene Hackman. When it came out that she was being paid a whopping $4 million for her role, things began to make more sense. Most speculated that the film had been in trouble, and director Jean-Claude Tramont's wife, Sue Mengers, just happened to be Barbra's agent. *All Night Long* follows the tale of George Dupler, an unhappy man in an unhappy marriage, who, after he throws a chair through his bosses' window, is demoted to working at an all-night drugstore. There he meets and falls in love with Cheryl Gibbons, who is not only married but already

Barbra once again gave a passionate performance as the main character in Yentl.

cheating with Dupler's son. The Gibbons character was a departure for Barbra, but her acting in the film is generally considered below her usually high standards. The film failed to find an audience, grossing less than $5 million. It marked the end of an era for Barbra, however. She ended her relationship with Mengers and embarked upon a new phase of her career, this time as a director.

And what a directorial debut it would be. "We felt it was a wonderful story for a musical...

because it is [about] a character with a secret," said songwriter Marilyn Bergman. "Throughout the picture, after her father dies, there is nobody to whom she can talk, to whom she can reveal her essential self. And this rich inner life becomes the [song] score." She could very well have been talking about the life of her good friend Barbra Streisand. But Bergman was raving about Barbra's obsession and next project, *Yentl*.

Barbra had first read the short story "Yentl, The Yeshiva Boy" by Isaac Bashevis Singer in

1968. She was so struck by the story—a rabbi's young daughter pretends to be a boy so that she can study the Hebrew scriptures—that she immediately sent it to her manager, Marty Erlichman, and David Begelman, her agent at the time. The responses were identical: this was not the type of story that American audiences would pay to see. Barbra was too old for the part (*Yentl* is in her teens in the story; Barbra was twenty-six in 1968). Despite the negative reaction, Barbra bought the movie rights to the story. Since then it had been percolating in the actress' mind as a project she would someday like to direct. She had read it to Peters during the first week of their relationship. Over the years she had hired many writers, including Singer himself, to tackle the task of translating the short story into a movie, but was ultimately frustrated with the results. As she had lived with the project for so many years, one studio executive told her that she should write the screenplay, pointing out, "You seem to know so well what it is you want."

By 1978 Barbra was a superstar with tremendous clout in the entertainment industry. She was the first actress on everyone's list when a new film project circulated around Hollywood. She was one of the most powerful women in Hollywood, yet she could not get a studio to finance this small motion picture that was so dear to her. Over the years, *Yentl* had been turned down by almost every major studio. A few times the movie had come close to going into production only to see management shake-ups torpedo the film. Finally, Peters, who was turning into one of Hollywood's top producers, signed a movie deal with Orion Pictures. The deal included a provision for Peters' company to produce a movie that Barbra would direct, which would of course be *Yentl*. But it would be almost three years before she would get her chance.

The beginning of the end was coming in Barbra and Jon's relationship. As Jon's star rose in Hollywood because of his commercial movies, his insistence that Barbra continue making the same types of films began to irk her. She'd been to the top of that field and had found herself wanting to stretch herself more as a person and as an artist. Peters persisted, trying to convince Barbra to go on a world concert tour, that it would be the biggest event since the Beatles came to America. But Barbra was determined, claiming that her long absence from the stage was due to overwhelming stage fright. Peters went so far as to tell her that *Yentl* would never get made if he did not produce it. As in every case when someone told Barbra she could not do something, this only hardened her resolve. And her love for Peters began to wane. Despite Peters' success, including the recent hit *Caddyshack*, starring Bill Murray, the studio got cold feet and ultimately rejected *Yentl*. It was only when David Begelman became the head of United Artists that Barbra found her studio.

Barbra's zeal to be faithful to the story's culture and religion led her to immerse herself in the study of Judaism. She joined a small Orthodox synagogue in Venice, California; studied the Torah; and helped her son Jason prepare for his bar mitzvah. To those who helped Barbra study and prepare for *Yentl*, she was exceedingly generous. Her gratitude showed in a grant to the

Barbra in her directing debut on the set of Yentl. It took her years to bring the story to the screen.

Hillel Center at UCLA for a Jewish performing arts center, and money to found a Jewish grade school in Santa Monica, California, later renamed the Emanuel Streisand School.

By writing, producing, directing, and starring in *Yentl*, Barbra was breaking new ground for women in Hollywood. Every move she made was scrutinized by the Hollywood community, which was apparently convinced that this was the culmination of an enormous ego trip. Yet to make the film, Barbra made many sacrifices in terms of her power and control over the production. With a budget of just $15 million, Barbra had to relinquish script approval, casting approval, and rights to the final cut of the movie. Even Isaac Bashevis Singer went public with his dissatisfaction. "I sold [the story] to a poor producer and he sold it to Streisand," he said in an interview. "Now she's found people who fitted the story to her desires. But the actor should adapt to the play—not vice versa."

Barbra cast the young actor Mandy Patinkin to play Avigdor, the handsome rabbinical student with whom Yentl falls in love. Patinkin also had his reservations about making a movie with Barbra, but after meeting her, he found his fears unfounded. "I was quite taken by how approachable and how caring she was about the piece, and about the material, on every level," Patinkin said. Amy Irving, who had made such a big impression in her role in the film *The Competition*, was chosen to play Hadass, Avigdor's fiancée. Although also reluctant to take a chance on the movie, Irving agreed after meeting the fledgling director. "She described to me things that I didn't read in [the script]," Irving said, "[such as] the growing of Hadass's character so that you could see she actually has a mind. Barbra took me though a journey that I eventually did in the film."

Yentl was to be shot in studios in London and on location in Prague, Czechoslovakia. Barbra's vision would finally be put onto film, but not without some deep-rooted fears. "I was so terrified for years," she later said. "Terrified of failure. I felt I could never do this thing." In addition to casting good actors, Barbra tried to surround herself with the best artists available, including cinematographer David Watkin, who shot the Oscar-winning *Chariots of Fire*. The company's arrival in England was greeted with malice from the press. Much was made of Barbra's history as an exacting and relentless perfectionist. The papers played up Barbra's "ego-driven" production and even took her to task for arriving with fourteen pieces of luggage

Barbra as actress in Yentl, plays out a scene with co-star Mandy Patinkin.

(despite the fact that the bags were for her and six others). Fed up with the constant negative barrage, the crew of *Yentl* sent a letter to every newspaper in London. In part, it read, "During the last three months of rehearsal and filming she has completely captivated us all. Though undoubtedly a perfectionist in her dealings with everyone...she has shared jokes, chat, and pleasantries each and every day....We have all worked with directors and stars who are the complete antithesis of Barbra Streisand but whose antics don't reach the newspaper. This letter is entirely unsolicited and is the result of our collected affection." It was printed in only one English movie magazine. Barbra later added that it was because of her multiple duties on the set that it was so harmonious: "Everyone gets along, you see? The actress doesn't fight with the director, the director doesn't disagree with the producer, the producer doesn't argue with the writer."

Yentl wrapped production in October 1982. Six months later Streisand was fighting to save her picture. Despite the fact that Barbra was paid nothing for her work as the screenwriter on the movie and received only the Directors Guild of America minimum salary for her directorial services (which she put back into the picture's budget), a bonding company was exercising its option to take over the production because it went $1 million over budget. "Please, we're going to ruin the movie!" she begged the bond company, "I'm going to die from the pressure!" The bond company gave her just six weeks to finish editing and scoring the film. Barbra knew that more than just her own reputation was at stake. "A man can fail and nobody says, 'We won't hire any more men,'" she said, "but let a woman fail and it hurts all women." With an extraordinary amount of will and determination, Barbra finished *Yentl* on time. She was emotionally and physically spent, and the weight of the world rested on her shoulders.

In a promotional frenzy, Barbra got her face onto the cover of several national magazines by the time the movie opened on November 16, 1983. The movie was a hit, and most reviewers raved about the film. "It's rare to see such a labor of love, such emotion in almost every frame of a film....Director Streisand has given Star Streisand her best vehicle since *Funny Girl*," wrote *Newsweek*. Some were less impressed, including the *New York Times*, which panned the film. But the audience came; the film grossed more than $50 million dollars domestically. Streisand had proven herself a successful director and producer, against all the odds and all the obstacles that Hollywood put in her way.

Yentl received five nominations at the Golden Globe Awards, including Best Picture in the Musical or Comedy category. The real surprise came when it was announced that, for the first time in the Golden Globe's history, a female was voted Best Director. "This award is very, very meaningful to me and I'm very proud, because it also represents, I hope, new opportunities for so many talented women to try to make their dreams realities, as I did," Barbra said when she accepted her award. However, when the Academy Award nominations were announced the following month, *Yentl* was almost completely overlooked. Only Amy Irving was nominated, for Best Supporting Actress. No Best Picture, no Best Director—it was a slap in the face that every woman in Hollywood could empathize with. Outside the awards ceremony, protesters waived placards proclaiming the

Academy a male chauvinist organization. *People* magazine devoted an article to the snub, with explanations ranging from "Hollywood is sexist" to "Hollywood hates Barbra." Whatever the reasons, Barbra could take comfort from the fact that there was so much attention being paid to the fact that her directorial debut wasn't nominated for an Academy Award.

With the sucess of *Yentl*, Barbra's career had taken a new and important turn. She had established herself not only as a major performing artist, but now as a serious film director as well. Her personal life had also changed; she and Jon Peters, perhaps the one true love of her life, had split up for good. "We reached a point in our lives where we both had to go in separate directions," Peters would say of the breakup. "[*Yentl*] was Barbra's statement and [it offered her the] ability to be completely autonomous and make her own decisions. I don't think she chose between me and the film; she chose the film and then it was time for us to separate."

SEVEN

Prince of Tides

H er relationship with Jon Peters officially over, Barbra was once again free to date, and she had no shortage of offers for her affections. Her romantic interests ran the gamut after the breakup, sharing only one common thread: they were all exceedingly wealthy men. She was seen with actor Richard Gere, businessman Richard Cohen, producers Arnon Milchan and Dodi Fayed, and again Pierre Trudeau. But it was the tall, dark, and handsome Richard Baskin who captured Barbra's heart.

Baskin was enormously wealthy, since he was the heir to the Baskin-Robbins ice cream fortune, but he was also an accomplished movie-musical director. He had even written several songs for the film *Nashville*, one of which he performed himself on *Saturday Night Live*. Barbra and Richard met at a Christmas party in 1983. He said he loved *Yentl* and she said she loved his coffee ice cream. They began dating soon after, and by the summer of 1984, their relationship was quite serious.

Love was not the only thing on Barbra's agenda in 1984. She watched her son, Jason, graduate from high school in June. She financed a movie entitled *It's Up to You*, which seventeen-year-old Jason directed and produced. The film starred Barbra's mother, her sister, and her ex-husband. She also pursued academia, auditing a class on human sexuality at the University of Southern California. She was escorted into the classroom after the lecture began and out immediately when it was over, wearing dark glasses and a hat and sitting in the back of the room in order not to be disturbed. She went on to endow the Streisand Chair of Intimacy and Sexuality through a large donation to the university.

She also released a new album, *Emotion*, on which Barbra included Baskin, along with herself, as a producer. (Ultimately, there were nine producers credited on the recording.) While her previous album *Memories* (1981) sold more than three million copies, it contained only two new songs, one of which was her classic rendition of "Memory" from the musical *Cats*. The new album was all-new material and another attempt by Barbra to create a pop sound. *Emotion* did sell two million copies, but it reached only number nineteen on the charts, her lowest-charting studio album since *What About Today?* Barbra's highly publicized first music videos aired on MTV; one was an artsy six minutes for "Left in the Dark." The other had her dancing around in several different costumes while singing "Emotion." Still, none of the singles from the album caught on. Moreover, *Emotion* was met with extremely harsh criticism.

Page 92: At the 1986 Grammy Awards, Barbra won an award for Best Pop Vocal Performance for The Broadway Album.

Page 93: Barbra arrives at the Beverly Hills Hilton for the 1991 Academy Awards.

At the 1992 Golden Globe awards with beau Richard Baskin.

The *San Francisco Chronicle's* Joel Selvin went so far as to say, "There are people out there who respect Streisand as an artist, but this could cure them." *USA Today* critic John Milward, a more sympathetic writer, urged Streisand to return to her Broadway roots.

"I had to stop recording songs that any number of people could sing as well as, if not better than, I could," Barbra recalled of the genesis of her next album. And who could possibly sing a compilation of Broadway show tunes better than Streisand? For *The*

Broadway Album, Barbra pulled out all the stops, even calling in the legendary composer Stephen Sondheim to tailor some of his classic lyrics more to her taste. She brought in Peter Matz, the arranger of her very first recording, to work as a producer on the album. (Naturally, her boyfriend, Richard Baskin, produced a couple of the tracks.) She hired the acclaimed motion picture director William Friedkin (*The Exorcist, The French Connection*) to direct the music video for the song "Somewhere."

Barbra sings for invited guests at her estate in California. Filmed for HBO, the concert featured such hits as "People," "The Way We Where," and "Somewhere."

Barbra's efforts to make the album a huge success paid off, both commercially and critically. Released in November 1985, *The Broadway Album* took less than two months to climb to number one on the charts, where it stayed for three weeks. The recording sold three million copies and was nominated for three Grammys, winning Barbra her eighth award, for Best Pop Female Vocal Performance. To date, *The Broadway Album* remains the most financially successful recording of Barbra's career.

In the beginning of 1986, Barbra's contract with Jon Peters expired. She renewed her business relationship with manager Marty Erlichman. While Ehrlichman had produced several motion pictures in the interim, including *Coma* and *Breathless*, he was eager to return to managing his protégé. "She and I jumped right back into it like there had been no gap," he said.

In April of that year, Barbra celebrated her forty-fourth birthday. Her relationship with Baskin intensified, and he moved in with her. Careerwise, she appeared on the Academy Awards, presenting the Oscar for Best Director to Sidney Pollack for his work on *Out of Africa*. She graced the cover of *Life* magazine, along with Sally Field, Jane Fonda, Goldie Hawn, and Jessica Lange, as one of "Hollywood's Most Powerful Women." Still, Marty Ehrlichman was intent that Barbra return to live performing. Barbra relented, but refused to tour, choosing instead to use her talents for a cause she believed in.

In September, a host of major celebrities and other invited guests arrived at Barbra's Malibu estate for the "One Voice" concert. The event, sponsored by the Hollywood Women's Political

Committee, was to raise money for several Democratic senatorial candidates. The seating was limited to four hundred people at the cost of $5,000 per couple. The show consisted of an opening monologue by comedian Robin Williams, followed by the rare opportunity to hear Barbra perform live for the first time in six years. While Barry Gibb joined her on "Guilty" and "What Kind of Fool," the rest of the show was all Barbra. Since she was backed up by only a small group of musicians, Barbra's most memorable moments in the show were when she sang her haunting ballads, such as "Send in the Clowns" and "Papa, Can You Hear Me?" The "One Voice" concert raised $1.5 million, bringing in more when the cable television channel HBO aired it at the end of the year. *The Los Angeles Herald Examiner* said in its review of the television special that "Streisand's voice is still the best there is."

Meanwhile, Barbra was already working on her next film role. Claudia Draper, the central character in Tom Topor's stage play *Nuts*, is a high-priced prostitute who has murdered one of her clients in self-defense. She is also a woman who is violently honest, outspoken, and unpredictable— one whose "normalcy" could be questioned, but who is by no means committable. So instead of accepting an insanity plea foisted upon her by the court and her influential parents, Claudia chooses to fight to stand trial. In the course of the courtroom drama, the audience learns that Claudia has been abused by her father while her passive mother looked the other way.

Barbra was attracted to the role on two levels. First, she saw the opportunity to play a woman, like herself, whose shocking honesty causes her to be misunderstood. "That's what I love about this character," Barbra said, "She speaks the truth and she gets in trouble." On an even more personal level, Barbra's childhood, complete with the emotionally abusive Louis Kind and her mother who did little to stop him, allowed her to further relate to the character. Barbra later stated that the role helped her to "let all my rage out."

The initial problem for Barbra in playing Claudia was that another actress had already been cast. Director Mark Rydell (*The Rose, On Golden Pond*), while aware of Streisand's interest, did not want to hold the production schedule to accommodate the actress, so he cast the up-and-coming Debra Winger. However, when the project stalled in the screenplay process, Rydell took a break to direct *The River* and Winger bowed out of the project. When Rydell was free to work on *Nuts* again, he presented the

On location in New York City, in 1986, for the filming of Nuts. Despite the financial risk, Barbra refused to shy away from controversial themes.

role to Barbra, who accepted and also agreed to produce the project.

Rydell still needed an acceptable script, but his method of obtaining one proved highly unprofessional. He commissioned drafts from two respected screenwriters, neither one knowing the other was working on the same project—and then he went to Hawaii for a vacation. The screenwriters eventually caught on; both quit, and one of them phoned Rydell, leaving the message "After Hawaii, go directly to hell."

When Barbra learned of the fiasco, she played mediator, calling the writers and asking them to

work together to write a draft. After Rydell apologized, the screenwriters agreed to Barbra's proposition, and set to work on the script. Two drafts later, Rydell, Barbra, and Warner Bros., the studio financing the movie, were finally satisfied and the screenplay was ready to go. However, Warner soon decided that they were not pleased with the director, and citing "a number of factors," the studio ousted him from the project. Barbra tried unsuccessfully to rectify the situation, then found herself in the position of finding a new director.

Barbra realized that playing the volatile Claudia would not be an easy task, so she set out

Barbra as Claudia Draper, the troubled prostitute in Nuts. Claudia's trial was a vehicle for Barbra to express her feminist viewpoint.

to find a director who, like Rydell, focused on the actors. Warner Bros. initially approached Barbra and asked her to take up the task, but she refused, in part because she didn't want to direct again so soon after *Yentl* and also because she didn't want anyone to think she had ousted Rydell to make room for herself. Instead, she chose Martin Ritt (*Hud, Norma Rae*) as her primary candidate for the job. She knew she had found her man when she met with the sixty-

Barbra accompanied heartthrob Don Johnson to the premier of his film Sweethearts Dance.

eight-year-old Ritt and he questioned her ability to play the role. Claudia, after all, besides being outspoken, was also a $500-an-hour call girl, described in the play as capable of "spoiling you so bad you'll hate every other woman you touch." Barbra was not put off by Ritt's qualms; in fact, with his bluntness, she felt he would challenge her to stretch her abilities. She recalled, "He got my hair up and I said, 'Good. You're the one. It's a match.'"

With the cast set—Richard Dreyfuss as Claudia's public defender, Maureen Stapleton and Karl Malden as her parents, and Leslie Nielsen and Eli Wallach in smaller roles—the film was finally ready to go into production in October 1986. The film was completed about one year later.

Despite exceedingly positive word of mouth during previews, *Nuts*, which opened on November 20, 1987, garnered mixed reviews. While some reviewers touted Barbra's performance as gritty and robust, others questioned her suitability for the role, while still others found the whole film pretentious. *Newsweek's* review labeled it "a classic example of A-list liberal Hollywood turning out what it thinks is Important Entertainment." The lukewarm press combined with the gloomy subject matter of the film led to box-office failure. *Nuts* barely made enough money to cover the production budget, and lost a considerable amount in advertising costs. The film also failed to win any awards; while it was up for two Golden Globes, it received not a single Academy Award nomination.

Meanwhile, as *Nuts* was being finished, Barbra's love life changed radically. Her relationship with Baskin had evolved into a close friendship, and when the romance fizzled, the ice cream mogul moved out of Barbra's house. By the new year, Barbra was entangled in a new, extremely high-profile love affair.

The target of her affection seemed an unlikely choice: Don Johnson, the sexy star of the hit television show *Miami Vice*, whose face had recently graced the cover of *People* magazine as

"The Sexiest Man Alive." Johnson was a huge star at the time, eight years younger than Barbra, a recovered substance abuser, and a notorious ladies' man. He had been married to and divorced from Melanie Griffith, had had a long relationship and a child with actress Patti D'Arbanville (who had appeared in *The Main Event* with Barbra), and had reportedly engaged in numerous affairs with adoring and obliging *Miami Vice* fans. His lovers weren't limited to his own groupies—Johnson even had a fling with famous rock and roll groupie Pamela Des Barres, who raved about his sexual prowess in her tell-all book, *I'm with the Band.*

Barbra had met Johnson at the Grammy Awards in February 1987, but their attraction didn't ignite until December, when they met again at a holiday party in Aspen, Colorado, where both were vacationing. Johnson took Barbra by the arm and led her to a quiet balcony, where they talked and laughed the night away. She invited him to a New Year's Eve party at her rented Aspen chalet, and Johnson invited her to dinner at his hotel. When the vacation ended, the relationship continued, to the delight of the tabloid press, who reported every Barbra and Don sighting with great fanfare. Gossip columnist Liz Smith, when she first saw the cou-

ple together, ran a headline in her next article that read "It's Barbra & Don & don't say it isn't!" They were dubbed "Hollywood's newest odd couple," and everywhere they went, their appearance created a stir. When Barbra arrived at a convention in February 1988, to be honored as "Female Star of the Decade," Johnson was on her arm. As the conventioneers went wild, Jon Peters, who was on the dais, jumped down and warmly embraced the couple. Barbra and Don recorded a duet together entitled "Till I Loved You," which hit number seventeen on the pop charts and number one on adult contemporary venues. Johnson's album *Till I Loved You* went gold, while Barbra's LP of the same name went platinum. Barbra even did an unpaid cameo on *Miami Vice*, and a photographer on the set tried to sneak photos of the couple, prompting Johnson to physically remove the camera from the photographer's hands.

Despite rumors of marriage, the romance proved a whirlwind, intense and short-lived. In July 1988, Johnson reunited with Melanie Griffith, who had just completed rehabilitation for her own substance abuse problem. Soon after, Melanie appeared on *Miami Vice*, acting in provocative love scenes with Johnson. By December, Johnson had proposed to Melanie, presenting her with a four-carat diamond engagement ring, and by the spring of 1989 the two were remarried. (They later divorced again.) While Don's rekindled love for Melanie came as a shock to Barbra, she was wholly supportive. In an interview with the *New York Daily News*, Johnson said, "During one conversation I told Barbra about the affection I still had for Melanie. Barbra said to me, 'Don, in spite of your reputation, you're a family man at heart. You need a base and a family life. It may be that you've never stopped loving Melanie.'" Barbra remained friends with Don after his marriage to Melanie. Said Johnson, "Barbra is part of the family."

Barbra quickly found something besides a man to become passionate about: a new project based on *The Prince of Tides*, a novel by Pat Conroy. The story revolves around the character of Tom Wingo, the son of a southern shrimper, a football coach, and a man with a crumbling marriage, who travels from his home in South Carolina to New York to save his suicidal twin sister Savannah, only to be saved himself by Savannah's psychiatrist, Susan Lowenstein.

Barbra was intent on directing the work, which, like *Nuts*, explored the problems arising from family dysfunction. But in order to be able to obtain financing, and because she felt bonded to the character, Barbra also decided to play the role of Lowenstein. Barbra stated on one occasion, "I couldn't have gotten the picture made if I wasn't in it. I certainly wouldn't have gotten to direct"; on another, "When I first read the book, I thought, 'Jesus, I'm perfect for this part. I identify with this woman completely'"; and yet another, "I thought I was the best person for the role." While critics were quick to note that, as with Claudia Draper, the character description of Lowenstein—"black-haired," "breathtakingly beautiful," "airbrushed with beauty and good taste," "with the incorruptible carriage of lionesses"—seemed contradictory to the earthy Streisand, Conroy was thrilled to have her involved in the project. The author said, "I don't know how Barbra got the rights to *The Prince of Tides*, but I'm sure fate played some part of it. I listen to music when I write. And Barbra was the performer I listened to while writing *The Prince of Tides*."

Barbra pursued several actors for the leading role of Tom Wingo, a character who is extremely masculine, but who, in the course of the story, experiences highly charged emotions when he reveals his innermost secrets. While she discussed the role with several stars, including Robert Redford, Jeff Bridges, and Kevin Costner, she

Nick Nolte as Tom Wingo and Barbra as Susan Lowenstein in The Prince of Tides. Nolte's gripping performance played against his usual macho image.

found her Tom Wingo in Nick Nolte, who not only wanted very much to play it, but also wanted to work with a female director. Nolte said, "I'd wanted to work with a female director for maybe five years. I knew you'd get a different kind of insight." Barbra knew the instant she met with him that she'd cast him for the role. "I saw a lot of pain in his work, in his eyes. In talking to him, he was at a vulnerable place, ready to explore feelings, romantic feelings, sexual feelings, and deep, secretive feelings."

Her leading man found, Barbra was met with another obstacle to overcome. The financing for the film, through MGM/UA, fell through. The movie was brought back to life, however, through none other than Jon Peters. Peters had become co-chairman of Columbia Pictures. He offered to back the film, and after a bit of haggling over Barbra's fee, the deal became official—Columbia Pictures was to make *The Prince of Tides.*

The picture became even more of a family affair after Barbra's son Jason was cast as Lowenstein's son Bernard. Jason had asked his mother early on if he could play the role, but initially Barbra balked due to her fear of being accused of nepotism as well as her belief that Jason wasn't right for Bernard, an aspiring football player. In fact, she even gave the role to another actor, Chris O'Donnell, a handsome young man who had played quarterback on his high school football team. When Pat Conroy heard the decision, however, he felt Barbra was making a mistake. "That ain't the kid," he said of O'Donnell. Then he explained that Bernard was not supposed to be a good athlete. As Barbra flipped through pictures of other actors she'd auditioned for the part, one caught Conroy's eye. "That's the kid right there," he said. Conroy didn't know that "the kid" was

Barbra brought her son Jason onto the set again, this time as an actor in The Prince of Tides.

Barbra's son. After some cajoling on the part of Conroy, Barbra recast the role of Bernard with Jason Gould.

The production of *The Prince of Tides* commenced in June 1990. During the course of putting the film together, Barbra's focus shifted from her work on the picture back onto her own family. Three weeks into shooting, her eighty-two-year-old mother underwent heart bypass surgery. While Barbra did not postpone the movie, her attitude toward the project was altered. "When I was faced with the potential loss of my mother," she commented, "the movie became much easier. It lost its importance." When Diana recovered from the surgery, Barbra was filled with relief and a sense of good fortune. "I mean, the movie was only a movie," she said, "but how lucky I was to have this opportunity to have my mother still alive; that's the important thing—life."

Barbra had always been media-shy, and although she warned her son about the press when he signed on to play the role of Bernard, both mother and son (as well as ex-husband) were shocked when, during postproduction, Jason's face appeared on the cover of a tabloid with the headline "BARBRA WEEPS OVER GAY SON'S WEDDING." While the wedding

Barbra, the Hollywood Diva, at the Academy Awards in 1992. The Academy once again snubbed her efforts.

shoo-in for many industry awards. The film did win one major award: a Golden Globe for Nick Nolte's performance. While Barbra was nominated for a Director's Guild Award, she lost to Jonathan Demme for his work on *The Silence of the Lambs*. *The Prince of Tides* was nominated for seven Academy Awards, but did not win any. *The Silence of the Lambs* swept the Oscars, winning in all the major categories. Though her film was included in the Best Picture category, Barbra even failed to receive a nomination for Best Director.

The National Organization for Women cited the snub as yet another example of Hollywood's sexist attitude—after all, no American woman has ever even been nominated for an Oscar in directing. However, columnist Liz Smith had another explanation for Streisand's exclusion, which was shared by many observers and which she summed up in an article written prior to the nominations: "Hollywood won't give Barbra another Oscar. They hate her. The movie community thinks she is selfish and impossible."

The Prince of Tides went on to take in large amounts of money at the box office, grossing $90 million domestically and making it Barbra's second most profitable film after *A Star Is Born*. Whatever the Hollywood community thought of Barbra Streisand, her public certainly did not agree.

story was a complete fabrication, the public "outing" caused Jason a great deal of trauma. Barbra accepted Jason's sexual preference from the outset, and even responded to the newspaper's claim by saying, "I don't care if my son marries a chimpanzee, I would be at the wedding," and described the article as "a new low in rag journalism."

Jason's work on the film, however, was quite successful. *The Prince of Tides*, which premiered in New York on December 9, 1991, was met with overwhelmingly positive reviews and hailed as a

EIGHT

The Mirror Has Two Faces

Page 106: Barbra Streisand opens the first of three dates at The Palace in Auburn Hills, Michigan on May 15, 1994. The last time she had performed in the state had been in Detroit at the Cactus Club in 1961 for $150 a week.

Page 107: Barbra has always been a strong and determined woman, which has sometimes made her unpopular in Hollywood.

O n April 24, 1992, Barbra celebrated her fiftieth birthday at a gala party thrown for her by Jon Peters. Peters spent almost a quarter of a million dollars on the event, converting his Beverly Hills estate into "Barbra's Magic Castle" complete with jugglers, clowns, and magicians, and inviting three hundred guests and their children.

After thirty years of stardom, Barbra continued to reap the benefits of her enormous talent. In December 1992, she signed a multimedia contract with the Sony Corporation. The contract is reportedly worth $2 million per year for ten years in order to seek out and develop motion picture scripts for Sony, plus $1 million when she produces, $3 million when she directs, $6 million and 15 percent of the gross profits when she acts, and $5 million plus more than 40 percent in royalties for each album she records. The deal is one of the most lucrative contracts ever awarded to a performer.

Barbra was the first celebrity invited to perform at the inaugural gala for the newly elected President Bill Clinton. She had endorsed Clinton during the campaign and raised more than $1 million with her efforts. On January 19, 1993, Barbra appeared on stage wearing a pinstriped suit-gown with a long slit up the leg, and sang. President Clinton beamed as she performed, and afterward he came up to the stage to thank her. Her bond to the Democratic Party and its platform continues to be strong, and she has been active and verbal on many issues, including AIDS awareness and research, gay rights, women's concerns, and the environment. She was invited to the White House on several occasions by President Clinton, and during her visits, not only did she attend many high-profile political events, but she also slept in the family quarters.

When she wasn't in Washington cavorting with Chiefs of Staff, she was attending tennis matches to cheer on an impresario of an entirely different sort, her new friend, tennis superstar and heartthrob Andre Agassi. When she was spotted at the 1992 U.S. Open in Agassi's company, and was seen during the match looking at Andre, as one sports commentator described it, like "an ice cream cone with a cherry on the top," she created quite a stir. In fact, when spectators started chanting her name between serves, Barbra got up and left the match, claiming later that she didn't want Agassi's concentration to be disturbed by the commotion her presence caused. The relationship raised many eyebrows. Although Agassi was a multimillionaire like Barbra, he was also twenty-three at the time, twenty-eight years younger than Barbra and four years younger

Far left: Barbra performed at the inaugural gala for President Bill Clinton, in January 1993.

Left: The Actress meets the President—again. Barbra hugs President Clinton in 1993.

than her son. The two had met in the spring of 1992 after Andre had phoned Barbra to tell her how much he had been moved by *The Prince of Tides*. Afterward, they went out to dinner and became instant friends. Barbra said of Agassi, "He's very intelligent, very, very sensitive, very evolved—more than his linear years. And he's an extraordinary human being. He plays like a Zen master." In June 1993, at Wimbledon, Barbra appeared to cheer on Andre as he played Pete

Sampras in the quarterfinals. When Agassi lost the match, Barbra was in tears. That was the last time Barbra was spotted as Agassi's companion at one of his matches. The extent of the relationship between Barbra and Andre, whether it went beyond a friendship, is not really known. Agassi himself summed it up by saying, "She's my version of a friend. I've been learning about the sweet mysteries of life and this is one of them. I'm not sure I can fully explain. Maybe she can't

With tennis super-
star and speculated
boyfriend, Andre
Agassi. Despite
much innuendo, the
two claim they never
consummated their
relationship.

either....We came from completely different worlds, and we collided, and we knew we wanted to be in each other's company right then."

During the Wimbledon match, Barbra's album *Back to Broadway*, the long-awaited followup to *The Broadway Album*, was released. The album proved an overwhelming success, selling 120,000 copies in its first week and becoming the first Streisand album ever to debut on the charts at number one. She also recorded a track of the song "I've Got a Crush on You" for a duet with Frank Sinatra (both recorded separately), to appear on his album entitled *Duets*. That album debuted at number two on the charts.

With all her successes, it would hardly seem possible that Barbra was short on cash, but that was the case. Most of her wealth was tied up in real estate and other investments, many of which had lost value by 1993. Since 1987 she had been trying, without success, to sell her Malibu property, which was valued at about $15 million and on which she paid $200,000 in property taxes each year. She finally donated the property to the state of California for a tax deduction. (She later auctioned off a selection of her furniture, art, and other collectibles for a whopping $5.3 million.) So when her old friend Barry Dennen suggested Barbra might solve her financial woes by touring live, which she hadn't done in more than twenty years, Barbra seriously considered the proposition.

When word went out that Barbra Streisand was thinking of performing again, only a brief moment passed before she recieved an offer she couldn't refuse. Entrepreneur Kirk Kerkorkian needed a huge act to open his new Las Vegas megahotel venture, the MGM Grand. He never even considered anyone besides Barbra, and when he came to her with an offer of ninety percent of the gross, which he estimated at $10 million, for two nights of work, Barbra graciously acquiesced. Not only did the money appeal to her, but so did the opportunity to see if she had overcome her stage fright to the point that she could pursue a live touring venture again.

On December 31, 1993, Streisand fans from all over the world filled every seat of the MGM Grand's arena, seats for which they had paid a minimum of $100. Beautiful and elegant, Barbra swept onto the stage in front of a breathless crowd. From the moment she began to sing the strains of "Happy Days Are Here Again," Barbra dazzled her audience and convinced herself that she could still delight a crowd of thirty thousand adoring fans. At the end of the concert, Barbra turned to Marvin Hamlisch, who conducted the

In concert at Wembley stadium, one stop on her triumphant return to live performance.

sixty-four piece orchestra that backed her up, and exclaimed, "I did it! I did it!" The two concerts proved a resounding success, grossing more than $13 million in ticket sales and garnering excellent reviews from even Barbra's harshest critics.

In January 1994, the announcement was made by Marty Ehrlichman: Barbra Streisand was going to stage a three-month tour of Europe and the United States. After twenty-eight years, Barbra Streisand was going on tour again. The first scheduled concert dates were set for April at Wembley Stadium in London, the only European city Barbra would visit. Tickets went

Right: Streisand was escorted by television news anchor Peter Jennings at the White House.

Far right: With fashion designer Donna Karan, at the twelfth annual Council of Fashion Designers Award gala in New York in 1993.

on sale in March in five U.S. cities with top ticket prices of $350. The shows in both the U.S. and U.K. sold out immediately. Scalpers went on to obtain up to $5,000 for a single ticket.

Barbra's performance thrilled audiences in every venue. In London, Prince Charles, heir to the British throne, came backstage to congratulate her and express his long-held admiration for the performer he has referred to as "my only pin-up." In Washington, D.C., she performed for an audience that, of course, included the President and First Lady. One Washington reviewer referred to her as "the First Voice." In Detroit, Barbra brought down the house, despite

the fact that she was performing with a 102° fever. Her illness forced her to postpone the first four of her six Anaheim, California, dates. Two weeks later, still ailing, she opened in Anaheim. *The Orange County Register* said of her performance, "In a dazzling, multimedia tour de force, La Streisand showed the audience why she is so worthy of all the hoopla." She was driven in a Winnebago to her next engagement in San Jose, California, because she had a bad feeling about flying, then, overcoming her paranoia, flew to the White House after her performances for a state dinner, to which she was escorted by news anchor Peter Jennings.

Streisand appeared on the giant Sony Jumbotron in Times Square while performing "Somewhere" live at Madison Square Garden on July 22, 1994.

Her seven shows in Madison Square Garden in New York City grossed more than $60 million, which made the stand, according to *Billboard* magazine, "the largest grossing engagement in American music history." Her final encore in New York City, "Somewhere," was broadcast on the Jumbotron overlooking Times Square for the thousands of fans who had gathered to hear their idol.

In Anaheim, California, the last concert of what Barbra had stated would be her final tour took place on July 24, 1994. While the audience stomped, clapped, and cheered in a thunderous standing ovation, Barbra leaned down to an old

woman in the second row and quietly asked, "Are you proud of me now, Mama?"

The last two dates of the tour were taped for two separate television specials. Also resulting from her live shows were the albums *Barbra: The Concert* and *Highlights from Barbra: The Concert*. After the tour, Barbra delivered a speech at Harvard University on "The Artist as Citizen," and received an honorary doctorate from Brandeis University. She co-produced the television movie *Serving in Silence: The Margarethe Cammermeyer Story*, which was the true story of a woman who was ousted from the U.S. Army when it was learned she was a lesbian.

Barbra's film, *The Mirror Has Two Faces*, which was released in 1996, was a return to com-

edy. "I wanted to do a story with a happy ending," Barbra said. The story of an ugly-duckling university professor who falls for an inept but dreamy colleague (played by Jeff Bridges) was a marked departure from Barbra's other recent work, which was much more serious.

The film's other co-stars included Lauren Bacall and Mimi Rogers, who play Barbra's appearance-obsessed mother and sister, respectively. *The Mirror Has Two Faces*, received decidedly mixed reviews, with some calling the movie self-indulgent and others applauding Barbra's return to comedy.

At about the same time as *The Mirror Has Two Faces* opened, Barbra was seen in the company of a new beau, actor James Brolin. Brolin, the star of

Far left: With Jeff Bridges in The Mirror Has Two Faces, her return to "stories with happy endings."

Left: With boyfreind James Brolin at the the premier of The Mirror Has Two Faces in 1996.

such television series as *Marcus Welby, M.D.* and *Hotel*, met Barbra at a party given by none other than Jon Peters.

On June 6, 1995, she appeared on CNN's *Larry King Live*, and revealed what, to her, was missing in her life, a life that seems so complete. "I have had love and passion," she said. "I want a partner." She added later, "I wish I could have more peace in my life. I wish I could get less angry. I wish I could transcend certain feelings."

Barbra Streisand is a tour de force. From her early success to her superstardom she has remained a unique figure, hated by some, envied by others, always controversial, and adored by millions of fans. Besides being a consummate performer, both in acting and in singing, she is an accomplished

director and a political activist. Moreover, she is a cultural icon. People have copied her attire, her makeup, and her hairstyles, and some even try to capture the elusive quality of her magical voice. As in the cases of Elvis Presley and Marilyn Monroe, there are Streisand impersonators. A Barbra enthusiast might sit at the computer and dial up one of several Internet websites devoted to her; visit her Malibu, California, estate, which is now open to the public; or peruse the items on display in San Francisco, California's "Hello Gorgeous," a museum consisting solely of Streisand memorabilia. In a brilliant career that has spanned more than one-third of a century, Barbra Streisand has transcended stardom. She has earned herself the right to be called a legend.

Filmography

Funny Girl. Columbia Pictures, 1968.

Hello, Dolly! Twentieth Century Fox, 1969.

On a Clear Day You Can See Forever. Paramount Pictures, 1970.

The Owl and the Pussycat. Columbia Pictures, 1970.

What's Up, Doc? Warner Bros., 1972.

Up the Sandbox. First Artists, 1972.

The Way We Were. Columbia Pictures, 1973.

For Pete's Sake. Columbia Pictures, 1974.

Funny Lady. Columbia Pictures, 1975.

A Star Is Born. Warner Bros., 1976.

The Main Event. Warner Bros., 1979.

All Night Long. Universal Pictures, 1981.

Yentl. MGM/UA, 1983.

Nuts. Warner Bros., 1987.

The Prince of Tides. Columbia Pictures, 1991.

The Mirror Has Two Faces. Columbia Pictures, 1996.

Discography

I Can Get It for You Wholesale (Broadway cast album). Columbia, 1962.

Pins and Needles (Twenty-fifth anniversary recording of the musical revue). Columbia, 1962.

The Barbra Streisand Album. Columbia, 1963.

The Second Barbra Streisand Album. Columbia, 1963.

Barbra Streisand/The Third Album. Columbia, 1964.

Funny Girl (Broadway cast album). Columbia, 1964.

People. Columbia, 1964.

My Name Is Barbra. Columbia, 1965.

My Name Is Barbra, Two. Columbia, 1965.

Color Me Barbra. Columbia, 1966.

Harold Sings Arlen (with Friend). Columbia, 1966.

Je m'Appelle Barbra. Columbia, 1967.

A Christmas Album. Columbia, 1967.

A Happening in Central Park. Columbia, 1968.

Funny Girl (Motion picture soundtrack). Columbia, 1968.

What About Today? Columbia, 1969.

Hello, Dolly! (Motion picture soundtrack). Columbia, 1969.

Barbra Streisand's Greatest Hits. Columbia, 1969.

On a Clear Day You Can See Forever (Motion picture soundtrack). Columbia, 1970.

The Owl and the Pussycat (Dialogue and incidental music from the motion picture). Columbia, 1970.

Stoney End. Columbia, 1971.

Barbra Joan Streisand. Columbia, 1971.

Live Concert at the Forum. Columbia, 1972.

Barbra Streisand… and Other Musical Instruments. Columbia, 1973.

Barbra Streisand Featuring "The Way We Were" and "All in Love Is Fair." Columbia, 1974.

The Way We Were (Motion picture soundtrack). Columbia, 1974

Butterfly. Columbia, 1974.

Funny Lady (Motion picture soundtrack). Arista, 1975.

Lazy Afternoon. Columbia, 1975.

Classical Barbra. Columbia, 1976.

A Star Is Born (Motion picture soundtrack). Columbia, 1976.

Streisand Superman. Columbia, 1977.

Songbird. Columbia, 1978.

Eyes of Laura Mars (Motion picture soundtrack). Columbia, 1978.

Barbra Streisand's Greatest Hits Vol. 2.
Columbia, 1978.

The Main Event (Motion picture soundtrack). Columbia, 1979.

Wet. Columbia, 1979.

Guilty. Columbia, 1980.

Memories. Columbia, 1981.

Yentl (Motion picture soundtrack).
Columbia, 1983.

Emotion. Columbia, 1984.

The Broadway Album. Columbia, 1985.

One Voice. Columbia, 1987.

Till I Loved You. Columbia, 1988.

Just for the Record (Box set). Columbia,
1991.

The Prince of Tides (Motion picture soundtrack). Columbia, 1991.

Back to Broadway. Columbia, 1993.

Barbra: The Concert. Columbia, 1994.

Bibliography

Carrick, Peter. *Barbra Streisand: A
Biography.* London: Robert Hale, 1991.

Considine, Shaun. *Barbra Streisand: The
Woman, the Myth, the Music.* New
York: Delacorte, 1985.

Brenner, Marie. "A Star is Shorn." *New
Times,* January 24, 1975.

Grobel, Lawrence. "Playboy Interview:
Barbra Streisand." *Playboy,* October
1977.

Holden, Stephen. "Barbra Streisand Talks
(A Lot) About Fame and 'Prince of
Tides.'" *The New York Times,* 1991.

Jordan, Rene. *The Greatest Star.* New
York: G.P. Putnam's Sons, 1975.

Kimbrell, James. *Barbra: An Actress Who
Sings.* Boston: Branden, 1989.

Kimbrell, James. *Barbra: An Actress Who
Sings, Volume II.* Boston: Branden,
1992.

Pierson, Frank. "My Battles with Barbra
and Jon." *New York,* November 15,
1976.

Reise, Randall. *Her Name Is Barbra.* New
York: Birch Lane Press, 1993.

Spada, James, with Christopher Nickens.
Streisand: The Woman and the Legend.
New York: Doubleday, 1981.

Spada, James. *Streisand: Her Life.* New
York: Crown Publishers, 1995.

Swenson, Karen. *Barbra—The Second
Decade.* Secaucus, New Jersey: Citadel
Press, 1986.

Teti, Frank, and Karen Moline. *Streisand
Through the Lens.* New York: Delilah,
1983.

Waldman, Allison J. *The Barbra Streisand
Scrapbook.* Secaucus, New Jersey:
Citadel Press, 1994.

Zec, Donald, and Anthony Fowles. *Barbra.*
New York: St. Martin's Press, 1981.